TRAINING YOUR

PET HAMSTER

**Gerry Bucsis
and
Barbara Somerville**

Second Edition

BARRON'S

Dedication

This book is dedicated to all the hamsters that will have better lives because their owners read this book.

Disclaimer

The information provided in this book is designed to provide helpful information on the keeping, care, husbandry, and training of hamsters as pets. Any material, information, text, graphics, illustrations, and/or photos in this book may contain technical inaccuracies, mistakes, errors, omissions, and/or typographical errors, both in content and presentation. In no event shall the authors or publisher be liable for any errors or omissions with respect to any information contained within this text. Information found in this book should not be relied upon for personal, medical, legal, or financial decisions, and you should consult an appropriate professional for specific advice tailored to your specific situation. The information in this book is provided on an "AS IS" basis without warranties or conditions of any kind, either expressed or implied, including, but not limited to, non-infringement or implied warranties of merchantability or of fitness for a particular purpose. There shall be no liability whatsoever on the part of Barron's Educational Series, Inc., or the authors, for any indirect, punitive, incidental, special, or consequential damages, or any damages whatsoever, arising out of the use of, or inability to use, the information contained within this book.

Acknowledgments

Special thanks
- To our families for their support and understanding.
- To each other: for lots of fun times, laughter, and encouragement. We never have a dull moment when we're at the computer together!
- Thanks to Gary for his two-cents' worth!
- To the following individuals and companies for their help and cooperation:
  - Jason Casto, Super Pet, Pets International, Inc. (photos on pages 9 and 53)
  - Rolf C. Hagen, Inc. (photo on page 99)
  - Ron Leavens, Pet Valu, Fonthill, Ontario, Canada
  - Photos on pages 11, 46, 54, 89 (tl), (tr), and (b), 90 (t) and (b), 95, 107, 111 (t) and (b) courtesy of Gerry Bucsis and Barbara Somerville.
  - Photos on pages x, 12, 40, 43, 51, 57, 87 from Dreamstime.com
  - Photos on pages 33, 52, 58, 69 from istockphoto.com
  - Photos on pages 7, 30, and 68 are from 123rf.com
  - All other photos from Shutterstock.com

Note of Warning

This book deals with the keeping and training of hamsters as pets. In working with these animals, you may occasionally sustain scratches or bites. Administer first aid immediately, and seek medical attention if necessary. There are a few diseases of domestic hamsters that can be transmitted to humans, and some people are allergic to hamster hair, dander, saliva, urine, and/or feces. If you are at all concerned that your own health, or the health of a family member, might be affected by contact with hamsters, consult with your doctor *before* bringing one home. Always wash your hands thoroughly before and after handling any hamster, and observe a strict hand-washing protocol after handling any hamsters that aren't resident in your home. Some people have compromised immune systems and should not be exposed to animals. If in doubt, check with your physician.

Children should be taught how to handle hamsters safely. Never leave small children alone with a hamster, and never leave a hamster alone with other pets.

To avoid life-threatening accidents, be particularly careful that your pets do not gnaw on plastic, small objects, or electrical cords. Handle your hamsters carefully; they can sustain injuries if handled incorrectly. At the first sign of illness, take your hamster to a veterinarian. Also consult your veterinarian for advice on proper nutrition, care, and husbandry for your hamster(s).

Contents

Introduction

Rats, mice, gerbils, hamsters, guinea pigs—these days, small animals are becoming more and more popular as pets. And which small pet do you think is *most* popular? You've got it . . . The hamster. This comes as no surprise. You just have to look at a cage full of hopeful hamsters to understand their instant appeal. They're cute, they're curious, and they have big eyes and pouches to match. Best of all, these fluffy little creatures are virtually tailless, a major selling point for many people who are turned off by long rodent tails.

But hamsters have a lot more going for them than their good looks. To start with, they're inexpensive to buy and inexpensive to maintain. Being small, they fit into any house, room, dorm, or apartment. And, being quiet, they never annoy the neighbors. As an added bonus, hamsters make ideal pets for today's busy families. Are you out all day at school or at work? No need to feel guilty—hamsters sleep all day anyway. They don't get up until the late afternoon or evening, just when the family is on hand to play with them. Is there not much time in your busy schedule for bathing and grooming a pet? Don't worry: Hamsters are self-groomers, and they don't need baths. Even better, they don't need to be taken out for walks in all types of weather, a huge plus for time-strapped owners.

As you can see, there are lots of positive reasons for making a hamster part of your family. Now, are there any negatives? The answer, of course, is yes. There are drawbacks to every pet, and the hamster is no exception. Did you know, for example, that a good hamster habitat is time consuming to clean? And did you know that you should never disturb a sleeping hamster? If you do, it can get sick. So, when it comes to playtime, you'll have to go by your hamster's timetable, rather than by your schedule.

You'll find these facts and many more in *Training Your Pet Hamster*. This user-friendly book explains how to pick out a healthy hamster, how to care for it properly, and how to train it to become a first-rate pet. The book also describes specific techniques for teaching your hamster several behaviors such as coming on cue, using a potty, navigating a maze, and running an obstacle course. In addition, there's

advice on how to deal with problem behaviors such as gnawing and obsessive cage-bar biting. Then there are the fun chapters that get you interacting with your pet during playtime.

Many hamster owners don't understand their pet's needs, and as a result, their hamsters are left to languish in tiny cages without stimulation. Don't let this happen to your pet! Instead, follow the advice given in this book so that your hamster can have the best possible quality of life. After all, isn't that what responsible pet ownership is all about?

Chapter One
Choosing a Hamster Home

Before you buy

You might think that a hamster will be the ideal pet for your household, but are you sure? Do you know all the care requirements for hamsters? Do you know anything about their behavior? Do you know how long they live? Do you know anything about the different types of hamster? Do you have a realistic idea of the time commitment involved? If you don't know the answer to any of these questions, then you need to do some research.

Read books, surf the Internet, visit pet shops, contact breeders, talk to hamster owners—*then* decide if you're still eager and able to give a hamster a happy home. You are? Now be a responsible owner and get everything ready at home before purchasing your pet. First on the list is the cage.

A happy home

The big myth about hamster homes is that a small cage suits a small hamster. Forget this myth. The fact of the matter is that hamsters need as extensive a cage setup as possible. Why? In their natural desert habitat, hamsters range far and wide every night foraging for food—in fact, they can cover miles at a time. So, in captivity, they do best in a cage layout that lets them mimic their natural behavior. Buy your pet a home that provides room to roam, room to stash food, room for a separate sleeping quarter, and room for toilet duties.

If you try to keep your hamster in a 12-inch by 12-inch (30 cm by 30 cm) cube, he won't be happy. In fact, he's likely to get bored and stressed from inactivity. Prolonged stress can lead to health problems and a shorter life span. Constant boredom can lead to behavior problems such as biting when being picked up. It can also lead to obsessive/compulsive behaviors such as gnawing at the cage bars, clawing at the walls, and running endlessly back and forth. Avoid these problems by buying a habitat that gives your pet plenty of room for running around.

Too small a cage can lead to boredom, which can lead to obsessive chewing on the cage wires.

find on the Internet and on Internet classified sites. You'll also find lots of owner reviews on the Internet. If you read them carefully, they'll help you make a good choice and avoid a bad one.

The great thing about hamster habitats is that you can mix and match the different units and connecting tubes to make as large a layout as you can afford or find space for—the combinations are endless. But something you need to realize is that a single plastic module isn't going to provide your hamster with a large enough home. Think of two modules as the minimum, and add more as your budget allows.

The biggest plus with these made-for-hamster homes is that they've been designed to mimic the hamster's natural habitat. If you make the effort to link several modules together and customize them inside, your pet will be able to roam, tunnel, climb, burrow, and stash to his heart's content. (See the section called "Add-ons.")

If you can't afford a large enough cage setup right now, please postpone your hamster purchase until you can afford something suitably spacious. It's better to save up and buy the right cage than to make your hamster suffer in the wrong cage. After all, you want to give your pet the best-possible quality of life.

Hamster habitats

Hamster habitats are modular units made specifically to house hamsters. They're widely available wherever hamster products are sold, and they're easy to

When choosing a hamster habitat, here are a few points to keep in mind. First, make sure you match the habitat to the species of hamster you're planning to buy. For example, if you're purchasing a large Syrian hamster, there's no point in getting a setup designed for small dwarf hamsters. The living area is too small and the tubes are too narrow. You might think that a Syrian habitat would be great for dwarf hamsters since they'd have a lot more room to run around. But if you buy a Syrian habitat, your dwarf hamsters might not be able to climb up and down the larger tubes. Some owners get around this by arranging the tubes horizontally rather than vertically. A second point to consider is that large Syrian hamsters can sometimes get stuck in habitat tubes. It's good to keep this fact in mind when picking out a habitat, because some brands come with wider tubes than others.

A third point is that plastic cage units need to have adequate ventilation; they should have enough holes or slots for good air circulation. If you live in a hot climate and don't have air-conditioning, opt for wire or combination wire/plastic units instead of all-plastic ones. Whatever type of module you buy, make sure that the door opening is large enough for you to get your hand in to pick up your pet. Then test the door itself to see that it closes securely. And be certain to latch it properly each time you close it; otherwise, your hamster(s) will escape.

Another important point to keep in mind when choosing a plastic habitat is that some are better quality than others. A poor-quality one can be hard and frustrating to put together and take apart. Plus, the various parts can break easily when it's cleaning time. You'll save yourself time and money in the long run if you save up for a better-quality setup. This is where reading the reviews on the Internet can be very helpful.

A potential problem with plastic habitats is that some hamsters gnaw on them and make holes big enough to escape through. So, if you opt for a plastic home, check it frequently for signs of gnawing, and replace any damaged parts

immediately. (See the section called "Plastic-cage headaches . . . and solutions" in Chapter 6 for more information.)

Wire cages

Wire cages provide great ventilation, and they're easy to customize by attaching accessories to the cage wires. But are all of them suitable for hamsters? In a word, *no*. To start with, many wire hamster cages are too small. However, you can get around this problem if you connect two or more cages together. To do this, you'll need to select cages that have tube openings in one or more sides. You'll also need to buy extra tubes. Then it's just a matter of linking the cages with lengths of tubing. A multi-module system like this is a lot more pet-friendly than a single cage unit, because it gives your hamster(s) plenty of space to run around.

When connecting cages together, make sure that the tubes fit snugly and that they're attached securely to prevent any hamster escapes. This is especially critical if you own dwarf hamsters, because they can escape through very tiny gaps. Check the cage system frequently for gnaw damage, and replace parts as necessary.

When you're shopping for a wire cage, look very carefully at the spacing of the wires; if the wires are too far apart, a hamster can

A wire floor or shelf can injure hamster feet. Cover it up!

escape. For dwarf hamsters, the space between the wires should be ¼ inch (6 mm) or less. For Syrians, the spacing should be ½ inch (1 cm) or less.

Are you considering a multi-level cage? Then look closely to see if it comes with narrow platforms or with full floors. Platforms are a bad idea because hamsters have poor depth perception and can fall off them. Instead, choose a cage that has full floors on the upper levels. This layout is much safer for your pet. Next, check to see if the upper-level floors are made of wire or plastic. Plastic is the better option because wire can harm a hamster's feet. However, a wire floor can be made hamster-friendly by covering it completely with plastic mats made for pet cages, or with a piece of plastic needlepoint canvas. These coverings can be cut to fit and attached to the floor or sides of the cage with twist ties. For added comfort, and to discourage chewing, pile on soft nesting material.

It's not just the construction of the upper stories you have to worry about; you need to inspect the ground floor, too. Nowadays, the base or ground floor of the cage is usually plastic, but sometimes there's a wire insert covering the floor. Walking on wire day after day can injure a hamster's delicate feet, so you'll need to remove any wire insert.

Aquariums

Aquariums are readily available and can often be picked up cheaply at garage sales, flea markets, and Internet classified sites. You might even have an old aquarium gathering dust in the basement. But does an aquarium make a suitable hamster home?

On the plus side, aquariums are cheap, especially if you buy a used one. Also, hamsters can't gnaw through an aquarium, which is a real possibility with a plastic habitat. Another plus with an aquarium is that your pets can't kick their bedding out onto the floor as they can if they're living in a wire cage. On the downside, aquariums are not well ventilated. In the summer or in a hot room, your hamster could overheat or even suffer heatstroke in a hot aquarium. Poor ventilation can also lead to a buildup of ammonia fumes inside an aquarium. These fumes, which are caused by a chemical breakdown of urine, can cause respiratory problems for a hamster unless you're diligent about regular cleaning. Speaking of cleaning, another drawback to aquariums is that glass ones are heavy to handle and awkward to clean. Acrylic ones are lighter, but they're expensive, and they scratch easily.

Many owners like an aquarium for their dwarf hamsters: There's less chance of an escape! However, you'll need a large aquarium that provides plenty of floor space since dwarf hamsters need lots of running room. Some owners even buy an aquarium for a Syrian. However, most aquariums are too small to be a stand-alone Syrian habitat. Your pet will be much better off if you make a 10-gallon (40 L) or a 20-gallon (76 L) aquarium part of a larger cage system. How do you do this? You'll have to buy a special plastic lid that has two round punch-outs to accommodate hamster tubes. The tubes are inserted through these punch-outs so that the aquarium can be linked to a cage, a habitat module, or another aquarium. You'll need one lid for a 10-gallon tank or two lids for a 20-gallon tank. Can't find a conver-

sion lid anywhere? If you're handy, you could buy a metal/mesh aquarium lid—the kind sold for reptile habitats—and cut out tube holes yourself. Check the Internet for instructions and photos.

You can also find cage toppers that add an extra story to an aquarium. These certainly increase your hamster's living space, but unfortunately, they have partial platforms rather than full floors. A fall from one of these platforms could have serious consequences for your hamster.

A small aquarium, like a small habitat, is bad news for a hamster. If your pet is confined to a little glass box, he'll very likely develop obsessive behavior such as clawing at the glass, running back and forth compulsively, or eating the silicone sealant. Boredom for a hamster is a terrible thing.

Clear storage boxes

A popular, new way to house hamsters is to turn an extra-large, clear-plastic storage box into a roomy habitat. When picking a box, make sure it's very roomy with lots of floor space, and make sure that the inside is flat and smooth, with no raised edges that your hamster could chew. It's important to buy a clear box so your pet(s) can see out and you can see in.

You'll need to modify the storage box a bit to convert it into a hamster cage. Fortunately, this is a pretty easy job if you have a selection of tools and you're handy . . . or have a friend who's handy. Basically, what you need to do is cut away a large section of the lid and cover the resulting opening with ¼-inch × ¼-inch wire screening [6 mm × 6 mm], sometimes called hardware cloth. Next, holes are drilled around the perimeter of the cutout—support the plastic firmly while you drill, or it could crack. Then, the screening is fastened to the lid with small nuts and bolts, heavy-duty twist ties, lock ties, or small pieces of wire used as twist ties. Some owners also cut out "windows" on the sides of the bin and cover them with screening or drill ventilation holes in the sidewalls. If you do this, make sure that the holes are high up, where your hamster(s) can't gnaw at them and make them big enough for an escape.

Although large storage boxes are already roomy, you can give your hamster even more floor space by connecting two boxes together. Some owners even stack a few to conserve space. Either way, you'll

have to make cutouts in the boxes so they can be interconnected with tubes. Be very careful when cutting the holes . . . the tubes need to fit very tightly.

Add-ons

Add-ons are those extras you purchase to make your hamster's living space more interesting. They can fit inside the cage, outside the cage, or link cages together. Add-ons and add-ins include tubes and tunnels, connectors, ramps, mazes, balconies, solariums, lookout towers, burrowing tanks, wheels, spinners, teeter-totters, and tree houses. The more add-ons you provide, the more stimulating an environment your hamster will have. But you don't need to blow your budget with one swipe of the debit card. Save up a little each week and buy a new add-on when you can afford to.

When shopping for these accessories, ensure that what you buy fits what you already have—not all brands are interchangeable. Some items are made to clip onto cage wires; others come with suction cups that attach to plastic or glass walls. Make sure that the add-ons that join module to module are connected properly. Leave no openings for a hamster escape artist! And, whenever an add-on has a lid, make sure that the lid fits securely. Some lids snap/lock into place; others need to be taped down with

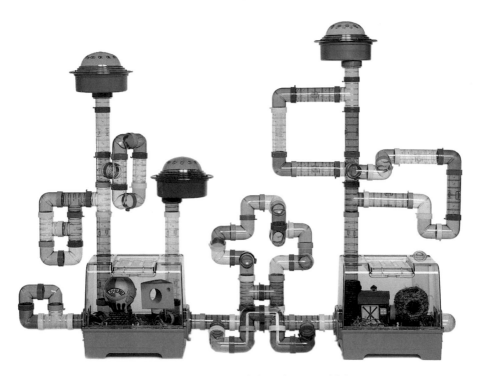

One plastic cage module is not spacious enough for a hamster. Link two or more together for a hamster-friendly habitat.

packing tape or duct tape to prevent your hamster from lifting the lid and climbing out.

Don't think of add-ons and add-ins as optional extras. They're necessary for your hamster's physical and mental well-being. Scuttling through tunnels, digging in a burrowing tank, running on a wheel, stashing food in out-of-the-way corners . . . all of these activities keep your hamster fit, healthy, and interested in life. This is another reason why you need an extensive cage layout for your pet; the habitat has to be large enough for the optional extras that enrich his life.

Location

Where in the house are you going to put that hamster cage? This is a question that needs careful thought. During the day, when hamsters are asleep, they need total peace and quiet. If their sleep is disturbed, they become stressed, and stress often leads to health problems. Although hamsters can clamp their ears shut when they sleep, they have a very acute sense of hearing, and noises that don't bother you will bother them. So pick a quiet spot for the cage. Don't stick it next to an entertainment center, a subwoofer, or

a TV that's on in the daytime. And don't vacuum around the cage when your pet is asleep. Keep it away from noisy, vibrating appliances like dishwashers and washing machines, and from appliances that cycle on and off, like refrigerators, furnaces, air conditioners, and freezers. The cage shouldn't be near drafts or a heat source, and it shouldn't be in bright light—this means no direct sunlight by day and no halogen lights at night.

These are the points you should consider for your hamster's well-being . . . now here is a point you should consider for your own comfort. Unless you're a *very* sound sleeper or you work the night shift, it's not a good idea to share your bedroom with a hamster. Hamsters are nocturnal; they're up and running during the night. You won't want to have your sleep disturbed at 3:00 A.M. because your pet is having a good workout on his running wheel.

So where is the best location for a hamster cage? No one spot is perfect for every household. Where you put the cage depends a lot on your unique home environment. The bottom line is that you should find a good, quiet daytime location for your hamster's home and leave it there.

Shelve it

Some enterprising owners have come up with a unique idea to provide their pets with an extensive modular system that doesn't take up much floor space. They put several cages on wall shelving, and connect them together with tubes. Not only is this a great space-saving idea but, it's a great way for owners to watch their pets at play. If you think you'd like to go this route, check out some of the innovative designs on the Internet.

Cleaning considerations

When you're looking at cage options, one thing to ask yourself is, Will this setup be easy to clean?

The biggest chore for hamster owners is cage cleanup, and the more extensive the setup, the more time consuming it will be to take apart and wash. But you can't neglect cage cleaning . . . it's one of your most important tasks if you want to keep your hamster healthy and happy. Hamsters *like* a clean habitat, and they depend on you to keep it that way. So what's involved in cleaning a hamster cage?

First, you need to clean the bathroom area, or areas, daily. This chore involves removing soiled bedding from any cage corner that's being used as a toilet, wiping out those corners with a damp paper towel, and replacing the soiled bedding with fresh bedding. If your hamster uses a potty, you'll need to dump out the litter daily and then wash the potty.

Another daily chore is looking for stashed food. Check under bedding, in hideaways, in wheels, and behind sleep houses. Hamsters like to cache some of their food and save it for a rainy day. If you're not vigilant about removing cached food, it can quickly become spoiled or moldy.

Roughly once a week, you'll have to clean the whole cage setup thoroughly. Depending on how big the cage system is, this can be a time-consuming chore, so your hamster will have to be temporarily housed in a travel cage or plastic storage bin while you get down to cleaning. Or, if your pet calls a modular system home, you could keep him in one module while you clean out the others.

First take out all toys, sleep houses, wheels, sipper bottles, and bowls. Wash them with hot water and unscented soap, and rinse them very well. Don't use strong-smelling soap or disinfectants that could irritate your hamster's lungs. Next, throw out or compost the used bedding, and wash the modules well. Now it's on to the tubes—a large bottle brush is a handy tool for this job. When the whole setup is squeaky clean, dry each piece thoroughly inside and out. Then reassemble the habitat, and put in fresh bedding.

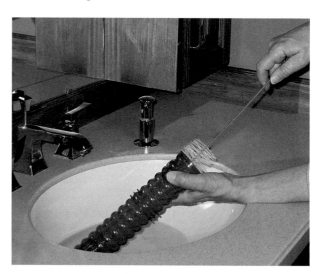

Chapter Two
Pre-Pet Preparations

Bedding do's and don'ts

Once you've decided on the cage system, you'll have to think about the bedding. For a hamster, you'll need two different types of bedding. There's the bedding that covers the bottom of the cage, and there's the soft nesting material that goes into sleep areas. For the cage bottom, what you want is comfy bedding that will absorb the hamster's urine. Although hamsters don't urinate all over the cage, the corner or corners where they do urinate can get quite smelly. So, odor control and good absorbency should come first . . . Softness is an added plus.

Wood shavings used to be the most popular bedding for small animals. However, a lot has changed in the last few years. There are many new bedding products on the market now, so it might take some trial and error to figure out which one is best for your pet(s).

Some owners still use wood shavings, but if you're going to go this route, stay away from pine and cedar shavings. These contain phenols, which are chemicals that can cause respiratory problems and possible liver damage in small animals. Hardwood, such as aspen, is the wood of choice for shavings. However, the problem with any wood shavings is that they're not particularly absorbent. Your hamster's cage could get pretty wet and stinky unless you clean out the soiled corners on a daily basis or potty train your pet (see Chapter 7).

Other wood-based products make better bedding than shavings.

For example, fluffy bedding made from dried wood pulp is a real winner in the softness department. It's also nontoxic, biodegradable, and more absorbent than shavings. If you pile it up 3 to 4 inches (7 to 10 cm) deep, your pet(s) can have fun burrowing through it.

Then there are chipped-wood products made from aspen or hard maple. These chips are absorbent and soft on the feet. Their only drawback is that they scatter everywhere, though this is not a problem in an aquarium or a plastic-bin cage.

For great absorbency, you can't beat wood pellets. In this category, pine is a possibility so long as it has been heat-treated to remove the phenols. Or check out odor-eating aspen pellets, which do a super job of soaking up urine and controlling odors. These pellets are not that soft on the feet, though, so for your hamster's comfort, you should top them with a layer of softer bedding.

Never use sawdust as bedding, even if you know it's from hardwood. It's much too dusty and could damage your hamster's respiratory system.

Pellets made from recycled newspaper are popular, too. They're nontoxic they're biodegradable, and they don't scatter easily. However, they're a bit dusty, and they don't do quite such a good job of odor control as the wood pellets. They're also hard on hamster feet, although some brands claim to have a softer texture. Other recycled-paper options are beddings made from paper crinkles or paper shavings. But whatever you do, don't line the cage with your daily newspaper; it's not absorbent, it gets smelly, and the ink can rub off onto your hamster's fur.

Bedding made from recycled cardboard is fairly new on the market, and it's getting good reviews. Available in either shredded or chipped form, it's soft, highly absorbent, and dust-free, and it does a good job of odor control. It's also nontoxic and biodegradable.

What about beddings made from grains and grass? It's best not to use these because hamsters can mistake them for food. Corncob bedding is a good example. Hamsters often eat this bedding, and

can choke on it or get it caught in their cheek pouches.

So, out of all the choices, which bedding is best for your hamster? There is no clear-cut answer. What you're looking for is dust-free bedding that provides absorbency, good odor control, and comfy softness. Keep in mind, however, that some hamsters are allergic to some bedding. If your hamster is wheezing or sneezing, showing signs of dry skin, has watery or sticky eyes, or has red or swollen feet, she could be suffering from an allergic reaction to her bedding. To be on the safe side, take your pet to a veterinarian immediately to find out whether she has allergies or something more serious. If allergies are the problem, then you'll need

to clean her cage thoroughly and switch to a totally different type of bedding.

Some hamster owners find that a combination of beddings works best. For example, you could put a thin layer of paper pellets on the bottom of the cage, and top it with softer, fluffy wood-pulp bedding. Or, you could put wood pellets in one module and heap up shredded cardboard bedding in another module for burrowing fun.

No matter what type of bedding you choose for your pet, make absolutely certain that your hamster doesn't eat it or pouch it. You don't want your hamster ending up with damaged cheek pouches or a blocked intestinal tract. If you see your pet snacking on her bedding, change to a different type immediately.

Comfy stuff for the sleep house

Now it's on to nesting material. Think of this as a cozy comforter for your hamster's sleep house. Hamsters don't usually curl up in a corner to sleep; they like a small, enclosed area for snoozing. Always have a sleep house somewhere in the cage. Ceramic ones are best because they're easy to clean and can't be chewed. Wood or woven grass houses are fine, too, as long as you're prepared to replace

them from time to time. Hamsters also like to hang out in those add-on sleep houses that are attached to hamster habitats. They enjoy the privacy and seclusion.

A coconut shell makes a unique, all-natural sleep house. If you're into do-it-yourself projects, you can make one by drilling a 2-inch hole (5 cm) in a large coconut, then scooping out every bit of flesh, washing the shell, and drying it well. (You can find more precise instructions on the Internet.) Or, for dwarf hamsters, here's another cheap and easy DIY project for a comfy bunkhouse. Take a six-pack, cardboard egg carton, close the lid, and cut an entrance hole at one end. If you leave a pile of nesting material by the entryway, your pint-sized pets can drag in some bedding in time for their next nap.

Sleeping quarters need to be stuffed with nesting material, because a hamster likes to burrow.

Paper products are a good choice, as long as you stick to brands that are bleach-free, dye-free, ink-free, and chemical-free. You could use plain facial tissues, sheets of toilet paper, or sections of paper towel. No need to tear up the sections; shredding the paper gives your hamster(s) something to do. Soft tissue paper and timothy hay also make good nesting materials. Plain paper put through your paper shredder works okay, too, although it can be a bit scratchy. A better option is to buy made-for-pets paper crinkles or paper shavings.

Although the hamster fluff available at pet shops looks cozy, it's best to pass it up. The same goes for fabric, felt, cotton batting, polyester stuffing, and cotton balls. These materials can be swallowed and can cause internal blockage. They can also get stuck in hamster cheek pouches, and the long stringy bits can get wound around hamster feet and legs. Avoid coconut-fiber bedding, too; the fibers are sharp and can cut delicate footpads.

Picking a potty

Did you know that hamsters can be litter trained? It's a good idea, because it makes cage cleanup much easier. If you want to give it a try, you should have a potty to go into the cage. See Chapter 7 for more information on store-bought and homemade potties.

Hamster nutrition

Before bringing any hamster(s) home, you'll need to have the right kind of food on hand. But don't worry; nutrition for your pet is pretty simple. For the main menu, it's going to be complete-diet hamster pellets. With these pellets, a hamster gets a well-rounded diet with each mouthful. Small-animal seed mixes are also available, and hamsters really love them. But there's a problem here. With seed mixes, hamsters can pick and choose what they want. And unfortunately, that's exactly what they'll do—they'll gobble up the fatty sunflower seeds and turn up their noses at the rest. When hamsters pick through a mix like this, there's a good chance they'll become obese and/or suffer from nutritional deficiencies. To provide both good nutrition and good taste, the best plan is to provide pellets on a daily basis and save the tastier seed mix to use as training treats.

Always buy small packages of pellets and check the "Best Before" dates. Hamsters aren't big eaters, so ideally, you want a bag with a long shelf life. When a bag's been opened, transfer the food to an airtight container and store it in a cool, dry place.

How often do you feed a hamster? Hamsters eat free choice, so pour some pellets into the dish and let your pets help themselves. They'll eat when they're hungry; they'll also pack their pouches and stash food in different parts of the cage.

In addition to the daily pellets, you should give hamsters a variety of other foods to supplement their diet. For a Syrian, this extra food should add up to no more than a teaspoonful per day; for dwarfs, it should be half a teaspoonful per day. Each teaspoonful should include tiny pieces from a variety of

food groups, because too much of any one food can cause intestinal upset or other health problems.

What foods should you be adding to your pets' diet? Protein-rich foods are hamster favorites. Most hamsters enjoy cooked chicken, turkey, fish, or beef, as well as cheese, cottage cheese, tofu, and yogurt. Scrambled or boiled eggs are also favorites. And for a special treat, why not bring out an occasional mealworm? You can buy these protein-rich treats at most pet shops. If you're too squeamish to hold one in your fingers, you can pick it up with tweezers.

Hamsters need some carbohydrates in their diet, too. Good sources include cooked pasta or rice, whole-wheat bread, and sugar-free cereals.

Fruits and vegetables are also sure to please. Hamsters enjoy vegetables like broccoli, carrots, celery, cucumber, peas, spinach, and zucchini. They also like fruits such as apples, berries, figs, peeled grapes, melons, pears, plums, and

strawberries. But no citrus fruit, please—your pets can't handle the citric acid. Avoid dried fruits, too— they have too high a sugar content, and they can get stuck in cheek pouches. When serving fruit, take out all the seeds, as fruit seeds can be toxic to hamsters. Any fresh produce must be well washed and free of chemicals. Be sure to keep the portions very small, because large helpings will give your pet diarrhea. And if you have dwarf hamsters, limit the fruit treats to once a week. Why? Dwarf hamsters are prone to diabetes. Their fruit intake should be minimal, because fruit has a high sugar content.

Grains, grasses, and herbs can also add variety to your pets' diet. Rolled oats, dandelions, alfalfa, timothy hay, clover, sorrel, and parsley are all good choices. Of course, all grains and grasses need to be herbicide- and pesticide-free. Can't guarantee this? Then a good alternative is to grow some pet grass. This comes in easy-to-grow kits that can be found in pet stores or on the Internet.

What about the commercial treats available for hamsters and other small pets? These should be avoided, because most of them are high in sugar and/or fat, and have little nutritional value. Also avoid made-for-people snacks such as cakes, chips, chocolate, cookies, popcorn, and pretzels. Hamsters will be healthier if you stick with protein, vegetables, fruits, and carbohydrates for their treats.

Now that you know the different types of food that can be safely added to your pet's basic pellet diet, the game plan is to make your hamster's daily supplement a mixture of several acceptable foods. For example, a Syrian's allowable daily teaspoonful could contain chopped cucumber and apple, a few rolled oats, a little bit of cottage cheese, and a few grains of cooked brown rice.

One last word on nutrition: To wash down all this good food, water is a must. Have fresh water available 24 hours a day. Are you concerned about the quality of your tap water or well water? Is it high in chlorine, iron, or sulfur? If so, you should provide filtered or bottled water instead.

Bottles and bowls

Hamsters need fresh water, but how fresh will it stay if you serve it in a bowl? Think what else might make its way into the bowl . . . food, droppings, bedding. In fact, in hamster cages at pet shops, it's not uncommon to see water bowls so full of soggy bedding that there's no water left. Don't let this happen in your pet's cage—buy a water bottle instead of a bowl.

Choose a water bottle with care. It needs to be leak-proof and gnaw-proof. To avoid leaks, look for a bottle with double ball bearings in the sipper tube, or a bottle that creates a vacuum when filled.

Finding one that is gnaw-proof is another matter. Hamsters can chew through plastic in no time, and a water bottle is a prime tar-

get for a bored hamster. Look for bottles with rounded edges—a hamster's sharp teeth can't get a good grip on them. Or, invest in a metal protector that shields the plastic bottle from hamster teeth. Pay particular attention to the sipper tube; it must be made of metal so it can't be nibbled.

There are sipper bottles made specifically for wire cages; these are attached to the cage with wire hangers or brackets. There are also bottles for aquariums, plastic bins, or the plastic areas in hamster habitats. These attach to the habitat walls with suction cups or adhesive-backed brackets. In some habitats, the bottle fits right through a hole in the cage top. This works fine for most hamsters, but the sipper tube might not hang down low enough for a baby or dwarf hamster. Always make sure your pet can reach the bottle and is actu-

ally drinking from it. When you get the height right, don't just hang the bottle up and forget about it. It's important to change the water daily and to wash the bottle well while you're at it.

When it comes to food bowls, a small, heavy ceramic dish is probably the most popular pick. A hamster can't chew through one of these or tip it over. Some hamsters have a habit of sitting in their food bowls, and this can lead to pee and poop in the pellets. Not too sanitary! To discourage bowl sitting, it's best to buy a small bowl. There's another advantage to a small bowl, too: It takes up a lot less space in the cage.

Hamsters are very meticulous housekeepers; they like a place for everything and everything in its place. So keep the food bowl and sipper bottle together in one area, well away from the sleep and toilet areas. And in an expansive cage system, provide more than one meal station so your hamster doesn't have to go far for a drink or a bite to eat.

Veterinarian visits

When you make a hamster part of the family, it's unlikely that you'll be looking at large veterinary bills. Hamsters don't need yearly vaccinations, they don't need neutering or spaying, and many of the medical procedures that are routinely performed on larger animals are not

practical for hamsters. However, like any other pet, your hamster can get sick and need medical attention. You should always have a hamster-care book on hand so you'll know what symptoms to watch for. With such a small pet, it's important to call a veterinarian the moment you notice that she's not looking or acting like her normal self. Don't take a wait-and-see attitude, as this could be fatal. And don't wait until your hamster is ill before trying to find a veternarian. Not all veterinarians are hamster specialists, so you should find one who is hamster savvy before the need arises.

Just in case a medical emergency should arise with your hamster, it's a good idea to save a little bit of money every payday. This way, you'll build up an emergency veterinarian fund and won't have to worry about how you'll pay the bills.

Chapter Three
Picking Out Your Pet(s)

Choosing a trainee

Now that everything is ready at home, the big moment has arrived. It's time to pick out your new pet. But where are you going to find one? For convenience, most people go to a pet store. If you're considering a pet-store hamster, it's a good idea to visit several shops. This way, you'll have a wider variety of hamsters to pick and choose from. In a good pet shop, knowledgeable staff will take time to give you advice and answer your questions.

Some prospective hamster owners prefer to deal directly with breeders. Breeders often specialize in colors and fur types that you won't find at pet stores. More important, breeders usually have a great deal of knowledge and experience that you can learn from. Also, breeders frequently hand-tame the babies. This is a big plus, because the earlier a hamster is handled, the better pet it becomes.

When buying a hamster from a pet shop or from a breeder, take a good look at the hamsters' living quarters. Cages should be clean and spacious, without too many hamsters per cage. They should contain suitable bedding as well as fresh food and water. Check to see that there are sleep houses in the cages, and make sure that the cage lighting is suitably subdued. Hamsters can get stressed out and sick if kept under hot, bright lights. Another important point to check is that males and females are housed separately. You don't want to come home with a pregnant hamster. And, you don't want to buy a pair of male dwarf hamsters, only to find out later that you've actually bought a male and a female.

Other possible places to look for hamsters include local animal shelters and Internet classified ads. There are many reasons why people have to give up their hamsters. Maybe you could find it in your heart to adopt a hamster that needs a new home.

Evening is the best time to choose your pupil(s)

Hamsters are nocturnal. This means they sleep during the day and are active at night. So think about it. Does it make sense to choose your hamster during the day? No, it doesn't. At best, the hamsters you're looking at will be half awake; at worst, they'll bite you for disturbing their sleep. Always wait until late afternoon or evening to pick your pet(s). At this time of day, the group will be up and about, lively and energetic; their true personalities will be apparent.

Does the species make a difference?

There are basically two types of hamsters sold as pets—the larger Syrian hamsters and the smaller dwarf hamsters. Syrian hamsters (also known as Golden, Fancy, or Teddy Bear) come in solid colors such as gold, cream, black, gray, cinnamon, sable, and white. They also come in variegated colors such as tortoiseshell (black and golden brown) and calico (black/golden brown/white). Patterns add another twist. Look for banded (white band

A Syrian hamster

around the middle), dominant spot (spotted), and roan (looks white, but is ticked with darker hairs). Then there are coat types to consider: shorthaired (sometimes called Fancy), longhaired (sometimes called Teddy Bear or Angora), satin (plush like velvet), and rex (wavy and velvety).

Although Syrian hamsters are what most people buy as pets, dwarf hamsters are becoming increasingly popular. There are four different species of dwarf hamsters sold as pets. The species that is most widely available is the Djungarian (*Phodopus campbelli*), which is also known as the Campbell's dwarf or the Campbell's Russian. Very similar to the Djungarian is the Siberian (*Phodopus sungorus*), also known as the Winter White or the Russian Winter White.

These two species of dwarf hamsters are difficult to tell apart unless you know what to look for. Although both species can have grayish-colored fur on their backs, the Djungarians tend to be more brownish gray in color. Both have white bellies, but the belly fur on the Siberian tends to be brighter white. Both species have a dark stripe running down their backs (dorsal stripe), but on a Djungarian, this line is thin, and ends about an inch (2.5 cm) away from the base of the tail. On a Siberian, the line is thicker and goes all the way down the back to where the tail attaches to the body. Also, on a Siberian, there are arches of darker fur on

A Djungarian hamster

Djungarian. Also, a Siberian has a patch of dark fur on its forehead. As for color, Djungarians come in a wide range of coat colors such as agouti, albino, argente, black, blue, chocolate, cream, lilac fawn, and opal, whereas Siberians come in a more limited range of colors such as agouti, pearl, and sapphire. The Djungarians also come in different coat types (normal, rex, satin, and wavy), whereas the Siberians don't . . . at least not yet!

In addition to the confusion that can occur because these two species of dwarf hamster look alike, there is confusion about which name goes with which species. Sometimes a Siberian is called a Djungarian, sometimes a Campbell's is called a Siberian, and sometimes both are called Russian Dwarfs. So how can you be sure of what you're getting? You might not be able to, unless you buy directly from a reputable breeder.

The third type of dwarf hamster is the Desert hamster (*Phodopus roborovskii*), usually called a Roborovski, a Rob, or a Robo. These ham-

either side of the body where the back fur meets the white belly fur. Sometimes the dark fur on a Siberian changes to white in the wintertime. However, this doesn't always happen in captivity.

There are other distinguishing features, too. A Siberian has a longer head and larger eyes than a

A Siberian hamster in his winter coat

A Roborovski hamster

sters are typically a sandy-brown color, with white bellies. They don't have a dorsal stripe like other dwarf hamsters, but they do have a distinguishing white patch above each eye. In addition to the common sandy-brown Roborovskis, there are also white-faced Robos, sometimes called Huskies. And some of these white-faced hamsters become much lighter in body color as they age. Although the color range of Robs is limited at the moment, breeders will undoubtedly develop a wider range of colors as these hamsters become more popular.

These Desert hamsters are the smallest of the dwarf hamsters. They're tiny, timid, very fast, jumpy, hard to handle, and hard to catch. Although they are endlessly fascinating to watch, they're not easy to hold, tame, or train.

The fourth species of pet dwarf hamster is the Chinese hamster (*Cricetulus griseus*). This species can be difficult to breed in captivity, so they're not always easy to find. They differ from other dwarf

A Chinese dwarf hamster

hamsters in that they have thinner bodies and noticeably longer tails. In fact, some people describe them as mouselike or ratlike. Nearly all Chinese hamsters have a grayish-brown back, an ivory-colored belly, and a thin, black stripe down the back. You might also find what's known as a Dominant Spot variety. These Chinese dwarfs have white coats with patches of darker color. The dorsal stripe is black, but is often thicker than the stripe in the common color variation. A very rare color mutation is the black-eyed white, but most people will never see one.

So, which hamster is the best bet for a family pet? If there are children in the household, go for a Syrian hamster. They're larger, not so quick, and easier to get (and keep) hold of. Being loners, they don't bond with other hamsters, so they'll be more likely to bond with you, especially if you work at it.

Do you have your heart set on dwarf hamsters? The Djungarian and Siberian dwarfs are slower than the Desert and Chinese hamsters, so they're easier to handle and train. The Robos are very small and fast; they're difficult to catch, let alone train. They are, however, good-natured, and some owners have had success in handling them . . . though it takes lots of patience. But it's probably best to buy Robos if you want to watch their antics rather than interact with them. Chinese hamsters, too, are very quick and timid when young, but if handled frequently, they become tame and affectionate.

One or more?

When you see hamsters at the pet shop, you'll probably see lots of them hanging out in the same cage. Does this mean that group living is the way to go? Can you keep three or four hamsters in the same habitat at home? If they are Syrians, the answer is a definite no! Syrians are loners, they are very territorial, and they must be housed separately. The only reason they're caged together at the pet shop is that they're young. For the first four or five weeks of life, Syrians can live in harmony. If they're left together any longer, they'll fight . . . possibly to the death. Are you still determined to have more than one Syrian? Then it's separate cages, separate playtime, separate everything.

The story is a little different for dwarf hamsters. Djungarians and Siberians are often kept together in pairs or small groups (same-sex, please, or you'll have a hamster population explosion). Roborovskis, in particular, are sociable, and seem to enjoy living in pairs. Chinese hamsters, on the other hand, can be aggressive toward one another. Although they can be kept in pairs when young, there's no guarantee they'll stay friendly when they reach sexual maturity.

Dwarf hamsters housed together don't have to come from the same

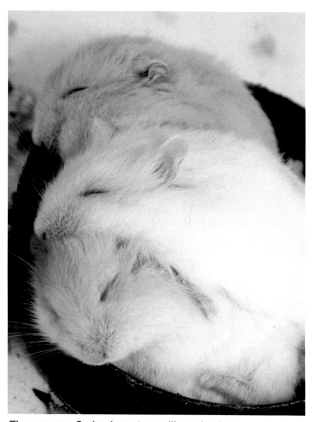

These young Syrian hamsters will need to be separated soon.

litter, but they should be roughly the same age and size, and they do best when introduced to one another early in life. Keep in mind, however, that a cage for a pair or a group needs to be big enough for the individual hamsters to go off on their own when they need to be alone. It's also better to have one large cage with plenty of floor space rather than a habitat that consists of several small modules. A modular system can promote territorial aggression.

Unfortunately, shared accommodations don't always work out. As they get older, some dwarf hamsters become less sociable and declare war on their former buddies. After eight or nine months—and sometimes even longer—some cage mates start fighting and have to be housed in separate cages. So be prepared for this possibility if you buy more than one dwarf of any species.

Male or female?

Do you want a male or female hamster for a pet? Does it matter? Not really. For pet purposes and for training purposes, there's not much difference between the sexes. It's the personality of the individual hamster that counts.

Some owners do feel, however, that if you're keeping more than one dwarf hamster, a pair of female Roborovskis gets along better than a pair of male Robos, and a pair of male Chinese hamsters usually gets along much better than a pair of females.

Young or old?

Most pet shops have cages full of hamsters at different ages and stages. Should you lean toward an older one or a younger one when picking your pet? If possible, choose one that's three to four weeks old, just weaned, and ready to face life on its own. When hamster/human bonding begins at this impressionable age, it's usually very successful. A young hamster that's handled frequently learns that people are part of its life. An older hamster that hasn't had this interaction usually doesn't become as tame and people-tolerant.

Trainability isn't the only reason for buying a young hamster. Hamsters don't live long. If you buy an older one, your time together will be short. If you buy a baby, you make the most of your hamster's two- to three-year life span.

Another advantage to buying a three- to four-week-old hamster is that it's unlikely to be pregnant; female hamsters can start breeding when they're just 35 days old. So, buy from a place where the staff knows how to sex hamsters, and where the sexes are kept in separate cages. Otherwise, you might end up with more hamsters than you paid for! In fact, before you buy any hamster, it's a good idea to ask about the store's return policy . . .

that there are no discharges from the eyes, ears, nose, or anus. In fact, any wetness and matted fur around the tail area could be a sign of wet tail, a serious illness that hamsters develop when stressed. Next, look at the hamster's teeth when it yawns. Make sure those teeth are not broken or crooked. Crooked teeth can cause problems with eating and mouth sores as a hamster ages.

Pick a pet that's lively and energetic rather than one that's cowering in a corner. Pay attention to body language—a hamster that's jumping around, stretching and yawning, sniffing and looking curious is a good bet. A hamster that's hissing or baring its teeth is not a good choice. Neither is a hamster that's showing any signs of biting. What you want is a pet with an A+ personality.

can you bring back any babies you hadn't bargained on? Remember, if you can't return them or find good homes for them, you'll have to be responsible for looking after them, and this could mean buying extra cages and accessories.

Of course, if you're adopting a hamster, it's going to be older than three to four weeks. In this case, just make sure the hamster is good-tempered and has been well socialized.

Pick a happy, healthy hamster

When buying a hamster, look for one that's healthy. How can you tell? Your choice should have clear, bright eyes and a shiny coat with no bald spots. Avoid any hamsters that are sneezing or sniffling. Check

Chapter Four
Handling Your Hamster

Hamsters can be afraid of people

As pets go, hamsters haven't been part of human families for very long because they weren't brought out of the wild and into cages until the 1930s. For this reason, hamsters aren't as comfortable around humans as some other animals are. Then there's the fact that the most popular pet hamster, the Syrian, is a loner in the wild — it's not part of its nature to form bonds.

What does this mean for you as an owner? It means that you and your hamster(s) probably won't bond overnight. You'll have to work at getting your hamster(s) to like you.

Early education is best

When it comes to training your pet hamster, "the earlier, the better" should be your motto. As you learned in the last chapter, a young hamster, three to four weeks old, is at an impressionable age and ready to learn. So start handling that youngster every day — several times a day — and your hamster will soon accept you as part of its life.

Hamsters that aren't handled frequently from a young age don't usually become people-friendly. Older hamsters can be taught to like people, but it usually takes a lot more time and effort. So if you're a first-time hamster owner or if the hamster is to be a child's pet, make things easy for everybody . . . buy a young hamster.

Homecoming hints

The day you bring your hamster home can be an exciting time for you but a stressful time for your new pet. Think about the move from the hamster's point of view. She's leaving familiar faces and places to go live with strangers in a new environment. And when hamsters experience change or disruption in their lives, they can develop a potentially fatal illness called wet tail. How does this happen? First, change causes stress; then stress upsets the delicate balance of the bacteria in the intestinal tract. This, in turn, causes diarrhea and then dehydration. If you see any signs of wetness around your pet's rump area, take her to the veterinarian immediately. But prevention is better than cure: To keep your pet out of the hospital, make her move to your house as hassle-free as possible.

First, give careful thought to the trip home. No handheld hamsters, please! The pet store will probably provide you with a cardboard transport box, but such a flimsy container might not stand up to your hamster's gnawing. You're better off buying a small-pet carrier for the ride home. At the store, ask for some of the used bedding from the cage that your hamster was housed in, and toss it into the carrier. Hamsters have an acute sense of smell, and if your pet is surrounded with familiar scents on the way home, she'll be much more at ease.

When you leave the pet store, go straight home—don't stop off for groceries, and don't drop in at a friend's house to show off your new pet. Your hamster won't appreciate the noise and commotion. What she needs is a quiet, peaceful car ride home. This means no loud music, and no loud talking. What you can do, however, is speak softly to your new pet so the bonding process can begin.

When you get to your house, take your hamster straight to her new cage. Of course, getting her out of the travel carrier and into the cage could be tricky. Your pet might be a bit upset; she might be fearful, and even defensive—in other words, anything but cooperative. So play it safe. If you've got a small carrier and a large cage (like a storage container), place the carrier into the cage and let the hamster come out when she's ready. If, on the other hand, the new habitat consists of

several modules and you can't put the pet carrier inside any one of them, then you'll have to transfer your hamster by hand. To avoid a possible bite, it's a good idea to put on a pair of gardening gloves first. Then, cup both hands around your pet's body, and gently lift her out of the carrier and into the cage.

After that, leave your hamster undisturbed. Go about your own business while your pet goes about the business of exploring her new residence. She'll sniff out her food and water, investigate the sleep houses, choose a toilet area, and perhaps even take a whirl on the wheel.

For the next few days, have patience. Leave your pet alone to get over the stress of the move. You can watch her explore, but no touching yet! Don't reach into the habitat except to change the food and water and to scoop out the soiled bedding. Don't jostle the cage, don't make loud noises near her, and don't invite friends over to look at the new pet. Do, however, stand close to the cage and talk reassuringly to your hamster at frequent intervals. She'll get to know you by your smell and by the sound of your voice.

After your new pet has been left to herself for a few days, she should feel at home in the cage. How will you know if she has settled in? When you see your hamster yawning, stretching, and grooming in a relaxed manner, you'll know she's happy in her new home. If you have a pair of dwarf hamsters, wait until both of them are showing signs of contentment before you start handling them.

DO NOT DISTURB

From the start, it's important to understand your pet's need for daytime peace and quiet. In the wild, hamsters roam the country-side at dawn, at dusk, and during the night; then they replenish their energy by sleeping deeply during the day. For your hamster to stay healthy, she needs to mimic the life of her wild relatives—she can't be programmed to fit into your family's schedule.

This means you should never, ever disturb your pet when she's snoozing. If you keep disturbing your sleeping hamster, she'll become stressed, and the stress could lead to health problems. In fact, the stress caused by waking a hamster from a sound sleep can significantly

shorten its life span. What's more, a rudely awakened hamster can be a grouchy hamster, and a grouchy hamster often bites. Don't blame your pet if she responds naturally to a rude awakening. After all, would you be bright and cheerful if you were abruptly awakened out of a deep sleep every night? Well, for a hamster that keeps night-shift hours, daytime disturbances are the prob-lem. So this is the rule for you and your whole family: Never disturb a sleeping hamster.

Here's another point to keep in mind. It's not just people that can disturb a hamster's sleep—house-hold noises can be a problem, too. Go back to the section called "Location" in Chapter 1 to refresh your memory about noises to be avoided.

Handling how-to

Just like you, hamsters don't always sleep soundly for eight hours straight . . . sometimes they wake up for short periods of time during the day. This, however, is not the time to start handling sessions. For the best chance of success, you should always wait until evening, when your pet is most likely to be wide awake and cooperative. How will you know if you've picked a good time for handling your hamster? Watch your hamster's body language. If she's cowering, hissing, squeaking, or grinding her teeth, postpone the session. If she's loafing around, eating, stretching, and grooming, go ahead and get started.

When teaching your hamster to enjoy being held, the strategy is to take things in easy stages. You can't rush your hamster into liking you. You have to build her trust and confidence, one step at a time. It's also important to realize that hamsters don't have the best eyesight in the world; they recognize you by your smell and the sound of your voice rather than by your looks. For this reason, it's best to focus on your hamster's hearing and sense of smell during handling sessions.

The first step in handling is to introduce the new hamster to your hand. Fingers that smell of food could invite an unwelcome nip, so before getting started, wash your hands with unscented soap, and rinse them well to get rid of any food smells. Next, try a little trick that seasoned hamster handlers use. Rub your hands with some fresh nesting material or bedding. This will mask your human scent, and will give your hand a smell that's familiar to your pet. Now, slowly slide your hand into the cage, taking care not to startle the resident with any abrupt movements. Rest your hand on the floor of the cage, and wait for your pet to make the first move. Hamsters are curious critters, and your pet is unlikely to be an exception. So keep still and let her wander over to sniff your fingers—this is how she files your smell away into her scent memory for future reference. If you chat reassuringly at the same time, she'll file away the sound of your voice as well.

Is your hamster a bit defensive when you intrude into her space? Are you afraid that your hand will be bitten rather than sniffed? It's okay to wear garden gloves rubbed in fresh bedding until you and your pet have learned to trust each other.

Keep the initial encounter short. But repeat it several times an evening for a few days, until your pet is treating your hand as part of the cage furniture. Now it's on to handling step number two. The next time you put your hand into the cage, don't put in an empty hand. Instead, hold a sprig of parsley or a sliver of chicken between your forefinger and thumb, and offer this treat to your pet. Be sure to keep your hand still, and let your hamster take the initiative. The idea here is to get her to associate your hand and your scent with good things. Repeat this step a few times each evening for the next few days.

The third step is to place the treat on the palm of your hand instead of holding it between your fingers. Again, rest your hand on the bottom of the cage. Now your hamster will have to climb onto your hand to get the reward. By repeating this step a number of times, she'll learn that she doesn't have to be afraid of your hand.

As soon as your hamster is willingly walking onto your palm, it's time for step number four. While she's sitting on your hand nibbling the treat, stroke her gently a few times with the fingers of your other hand. Chances are the little critter will be so busy with her treat that she'll hardly notice. When she's happy being petted, you can move on to step number five . . . practicing the cup hold.

Get your hamster to climb onto the palm of your hand as before, but this time, cup your other hand loosely over her body. Let her see that hand coming. Don't swoop it down from above or sneak it in from behind. If you do, she might think you're a predator and go into defensive mode (i.e., biting). What's the idea behind cocooning your hamster like this in your hands? Cupping her with both hands is how you get her out of the cage and how you hold her safely. But you have to practice the cup hold in the cage so your pet won't be frightened of it.

Wait a minute, though. What do you do if the cage opening is too small for you to get both hands inside? Is it okay to take hold of your pet by the scruff of her neck? The answer is no. Even though scruffing can be done with one hand, it's not a good idea. Hamsters have lots of loose neck skin and can easily twist around and bite the hand that holds them. So forget about the scruff hold. Instead, concentrate on cupping your pet with one hand the best way you can.

The last step is to lift your cupped pet out of her cage and cradle her against your body. When held this way, she'll feel secure, and she won't be able to jump from your hands and possibly injure herself. She might, however, urinate on your hands the first few times she's held. Don't be alarmed. It's quite common for hamsters to urinate when they're frightened. If your pet seems afraid, nestle her close to your heart so she can hear your heart beating—this works wonders to calm a nervous or skittish pet.

Does this handling how-to sound like a lot of work? Well, it can be. Although some hamsters take to humans fairly quickly, others need weeks to warm to their owners. Also, some dwarf hamsters, especially the Roborovskis and Chinese, are very fast and jumpy. It takes a lot of time and patience to get them used to being handled. But, however long the taming process takes, it's time well spent, because the more time you spend working with your hamster at an early age, the better, more people-friendly pet she'll be.

Teaching your hamster to trust you and like you is the most important training task you'll do. So be patient and be consistent. Before you know it, you and your pet will have forged a rewarding relationship.

Beware of heights

Hamsters and heights don't mix. Even a short fall can cause serious injury or death. So, one basic rule of hamster handling has to be *keep your hamster away from heights*. This means that when you're holding your pet, you should sit rather than stand, and the lower to the ground you are, the better. Sitting right on the floor is the best plan. But if this is too difficult for you,

why not sit on a footstool or on several cushions? Another option is to sit well back on a sofa. Then, if your hamster jumps out of your grasp, she'll land on the sofa rather than crashing to the floor.

Here's another good idea, especially for the first few handling sessions. Why don't you practice holding your pet in a bathtub? Put in the plug, spread out a flannel sheet, climb in, and sit down—you've just found the perfect practice place. There are several advantages to this setup. One, your hamster can't fall very far even if she jumps out of your hands. Two, she can't make a quick getaway because she can't jump over the sides of the tub. Three, you can alternate handling time with free-roam time in the tub. And four, she's right at hand when you want to pick her up and put her back into her cage. Tub sessions like this are a great way to introduce children to a new pet, especially a pet that can move so quickly and jump unexpectedly.

Even though you're being very careful, you could accidently drop your hamster during a handling session. If this happens, keep an eye on your pet for signs of discomfort. If you notice any limping, difficulty in walking, or change in activity level, take your hamster to a veterinarian right away.

Family focus

A hamster that's going to be a family pet needs to be introduced to everyone in the family at an early age. If you don't take the time to do this, chances are that your pet will bond with some members of the family but not with others. She might not tolerate being touched by anyone whose scent and sound she hasn't memorized. In fact, even if your hamster has committed every family member's voice and smell to memory, this doesn't mean that she's going to like every family member. Not all hamsters like all people equally; some have definite people preferences.

If your family is like most families, everyone will be eager to handle the new hamster right away and all at once. This could be a recipe for disaster. An overwhelmed hamster could start biting out of fear. It's up to you, as a responsible pet owner, to make sure there's no fighting over the hamster, no grabbing for her, and no passing her back and forth. One handler at a time should be the rule.

Of course, when a young child is handling the family pet, another rule should be to supervise, supervise, supervise! Hamsters are not lapdogs; they don't always like to be cuddled. But children are champion cuddlers; they tend to treat their pets like stuffed animals, squeezing them much too enthusiastically. This could be a problem in more ways than one. First, the hamster could be hurt. It doesn't take much of a squeeze to harm a hamster. Second, not many hamsters are going to put up with being squeezed. A hamster will likely bite a child if she's held too tightly. Even if she doesn't bite, she'll probably try to escape, and could be injured when trying to get free.

Older children, as long as they are reliable, can be taught the hows, whats, and whys of hamster care. But even then, an adult needs to make sure that the pet is being looked after properly. Is the hamster being fed every day? Is she getting fresh water? Is the cage being cleaned every week? It's important to check that children stick to their daily hamster chores after the novelty of the new pet has worn off. No matter what promises they make, most kids have a hard time following through with routine pet care, day after day after day. Whenever a child is looking after a hamster, an adult needs to keep an eye on things to make sure the animal gets the care it needs and deserves.

One of the joys of hamster ownership is showing your new pet to friends. Children especially get a kick out of this. But the question is whether it is a good idea to let nonfamily members handle the hamster. Well, certainly not for the first few weeks. During this time, the focus should be strictly on the family. Later, when you know your hamster's personality, you can decide whether or not her social skills are good enough for a nonfamily member to handle her. If your pet is calm, well behaved, and outgoing, then you can try introducing her to friends and neighbors.

On the other hand, if she's shy, nervous, or prone to nipping, then perhaps the best rule for nonfamily members should be look but don't touch. This is also a good rule for Roborovski and Chinese hamsters, which are fast and harder to handle.

After handling

It's not unusual for hamsters to urinate on their owners while being held. So, for hygienic reasons, it's very important to wash your hands after each and every handling session. But there's also another good reason for washing your hands after handling your pet. Some people are allergic to hamster dander and/or urine. Thorough hand washing after hamster-handling sessions can lessen this problem.

Chapter Five

Knock, Knock, Who's There?

You called?

In the last chapter, you and your hamster were getting acquainted. You handled him on a daily basis and your patience has paid off— your pet has learned to trust you and to feel at ease with you. Now it's time for the next step in training . . . and that is to teach your hamster to come when you want him. The idea here is to attract his attention without frightening him. If you just reach into the cage and grab your hamster without warning, he might turn around and grab or nab you. Why? He could think your big hand swooping down unexpectedly is a predator, and he could bite you in self-defense. However, if you teach him to come when called, rather than invading his space and scooping him up, he's less likely to be frightened.

Now the question is, how are you going to attract your hamster's attention? Hamsters have poor eyesight but an excellent sense of hearing. So, when you want your

pet to come running, why not try calling him by name?

Before you can teach your pet to come when called, you have to decide on the exact words you'll use for the command. For example, you could say "Come, Cosmo!" whenever you want your pet to come to the cage door or to your hand. Use these same words every time you call for your pet. Many hamsters catch on quickly; they learn to come right up to the cage door when their names are called. But what if your hamster pays no attention to you when you call his name? Or, what if he comes when it suits him and ignores you when it doesn't? Then you'll need to train your hamster, using what's known as the *conditioned-response* technique.

Conditioned response

What is conditioned response? It's a training technique used by animal trainers to teach animals spe-

cific behaviors. For example, a rat can be taught to run a maze, a dog can learn to sit up and beg, or a ferret can be persuaded to come to a squeaky toy. How does the technique work? It's really quite straight-

forward. You give a signal (the stimulus), and then you give your pet a food reward (the reinforcement). In the following sections, you'll learn how to train your hamster to come to you whenever he hears a specific sound. But before you get started, you'll need to find a treat that your hamster loves.

The trick is in the treat

Food rewards (or treats) work wonders when training animals. The problem with training hamsters is that they can't have a large number of treats in any one day. If you remember, back in Chapter 2 in the section called "Hamster nutrition," you learned that hamsters need a variety of extra foods to supplement their basic pellet diet. These extra foods, including vegetables, fruits, grains, proteins, dairy products, and carbohydrates, are what you'll be using as training treats. Syrians can have a teaspoonful of this supplemental food per day, and dwarf hamsters can have half a teaspoonful.

Since a teaspoonful (or half a teaspoonful) of food isn't much, you'll have to make it stretch into as many rewards as possible. To do this, cut each treat into very small pieces. For example, a cucumber slice can be cut into approximately 40 to 50 pieces. Of course, if you're holding out such tiny pieces to your hamster, there's the possibility that he could nip you accidentally when taking the treat. If you're worried about this, you might want to offer the reward from a plastic spoon rather than from your fingers. Another good way to deliver a treat is to put some plain yogurt into an eyedropper and squeeze out a drop or two as a reward.

Not all hamsters like the same treats. Just because one hamster loves cucumber doesn't mean that his sibling will. It might take some trial and error before you know which foods are your hamster's favorites.

Choosing a sound

Okay. Now that you've figured out your hamster's favorite treats, the next step is to figure out what sound will attract his attention. For many owners, a knocking sound does the trick. Knock gently on a surface next to the cage—the floor, the table, the bookshelf, the wall— or tap *lightly* on the cage itself. No hard knocking, please. Banging and thumping will frighten your pet and send him running to hide . . . just the opposite of what you're trying to achieve.

Another good sound for attracting your pet's attention is whistling. Store-bought whistles are usually too loud and shrill; they can be too piercing for sensitive hamster ears.

But your own low-toned whistle is fine. Other possibilities are a soft-sounding squeaky toy, or a glass or china bell.

The plan of action

Don't start on your plan of action until your hamster trusts you completely and will eat from your hand. And don't ever wake him up for a training session. Wait until he's awake, alert, and playing around or grooming himself . . . in other words, sending out signals that he's happy and content. Have the treats ready; then watch until your hamster comes close to the cage wires or to the cage door. As soon as he gets to the door, knock or

whistle and immediately give him the treat.

The timing is important. You have to give your pet the treat as soon as he responds to your knock or whistle so that he associates the sound with the food reward. At first he'll come to you because he smells the treat. But with repeated practice, the sound itself (the knock) will be the stimulus that persuades him to perform the action (coming to you), which gets him the reward (the treat). Eventually, he'll come running as soon as he hears the knock, because he's anticipating the treat.

Repeat, repeat, repeat

Knock-treat, knock-treat, knock-treat—every time you knock or whistle, make sure to give your pet a treat. And repeat, repeat, repeat. It's repetition that ingrains the behavior, and practice that makes it perfect. But always make the training sessions short . . . a few minutes per practice session will be sufficient. It's better to have several short sessions in an evening than one extended session, because a hamster's attention span isn't that long. Also, you don't want to overdo the treats.

When your hamster has mastered this behavior in the cage setting, work on getting him to come to you in the exercise area, too (see Chapters 9 and 10). After all, when you want to get hold of your hamster, it's a lot easier to knock or whistle for him than to go chasing after him. And, if your pet ever escapes from his cage, you increase the odds of finding him if he's been trained to come to a specific sound.

Chapter Six

Can Hamsters Be Trained Not to Gnaw?

Hamsters need to gnaw

Hamsters have four front incisors, two at the top and two at the bottom, and these teeth keep growing throughout their lives. Your hamster needs to gnaw in order to keep those teeth sharp and at the proper length. Because this is instinctive behavior, you can't train a hamster not to chew things. But here are a few strategies to limit the damage.

Favorite targets

What are a hamster's favorite targets when she's looking for something to chew? Almost anything in sight! Tubes, tunnels, exercise wheels, sleep houses, and toys are all potential targets. With this in mind, you'll have to think carefully about the items you put into the cage. Use ceramic dishes rather than plastic ones, put the plastic water bottle into a metal protector, or buy a flat-back style that doesn't

have any obvious edges for hamster teeth to get a grip on.

Be picky, too, about the cage furniture and toys you buy. For example, ceramic houses are gnaw-proof, but plastic and wooden houses are not. When you're checking the pet-store shelves or the Internet for toys, wooden and plastic ones are mostly what you'll find. Go ahead—

buy a few. They'll keep your hamster happy, and although they won't last forever, they're cheap to replace. However, if your pet is obsessive about chewing her plastic playthings, remove them from the cage altogether. Otherwise, swallowed plastic splinters could lead to intestinal upset and digestive problems for your hamster. Ceramic and wood toys are much safer choices, although the wooden ones will have to be checked regularly and removed if they get too chewed to be safe.

When your hamster is confined to her cage, there's a limit to the damage she can do, but when she's out of the cage for playtime (see Chapter 9), there are a lot more targets

for her to sharpen her teeth on. During any out-of-the-cage playtime, supervision is a must. Never let your pet out of your sight . . . there's no saying what she'll find to chew on.

Plastic-cage headaches . . . and solutions

If your pet calls a plastic habitat home, you'll need to check the habitat on a regular basis in case your hamster is chewing at the plastic. Likely targets will be connecting tubes, maze walls, the little lookout rooms on the tops of towers, and any part of the cage itself that your hamster can get a grip on with her teeth, such as vent holes or the edges of the cage base. If you do find any gnaw damage, don't wait until tomorrow to take action; it takes very little time for a hamster to turn a minuscule hole into an escape hole.

Is there any action you can take to discourage a determined chewer? The first thing to do is make a trip to the pet store and buy a bitter-tasting product made to deter pets from chewing or gnawing. Don't buy a spray because it evaporates quickly and won't deter a compulsive chewer for long. Instead, buy a cream or gel, which lasts longer and can be dabbed exactly where you want it. You might have to reapply the gel or

cream from time to time to reinforce the message. All of these products have a very bitter taste, but none of them will harm your pet. She'll just hate the taste of the stuff (well, most hamsters will).

Will this strategy work for all hamsters? Unfortunately, there are no guarantees. Some hamsters have oddball tastes and might actually *like* the flavor of a bitter deterrent. What then? Try another product. The unpleasant taste of herbs in one product might work, whereas the citrus flavor in another product does not. What if your hamster is overwhelmed by the smell of the creams or gels? In this case, you could try an odorless deterrent.

Have you tried more than one product and still had no luck? Then

forget the bitter gels and start a replacement program instead. Throw away the chewed accessories and replace them with something new. Look for a replacement that has a different design—one that doesn't have the same handy corner, edge, lip, or vent hole that gave your hamster the opportunity to chew in the first place.

Still no luck? Has your pet trashed the replacement accessories? Then your only option now is to minimize the use of plastic. Whenever possible, buy metal or ceramic accessories. If necessary, get rid of the plastic habitat in favor of a wire cage or aquarium. Of course, in a multi-module setup, you will still have the plastic connecting tubes. Does your hamster keep gnawing through these tubes? Then your best bet is probably to switch to a large storage-bin cage that doesn't have connecting tubes.

As for plastic tubes and tunnels *inside* the cage, get rid of these, and provide wooden tunnels/tubes or sections of PVC piping instead. Another possibility is to buy tubes made of edible vegetable parchment or nontoxic cardboard. These tubes are made specifically for pets and are okay for your hamster to chew.

Hamster teething treats

Your hamster is going to chew. And chew. And chew. There's nothing you can do to prevent this behavior, so it's up to you to provide her with something safe and owner approved to munch on. If you stock her cage with chewables, your pet will get the gnawing she needs and be less likely to attack her cage or cage furniture. Luckily, you can buy lots of colorful, flavorful, inexpensive, wooden hamster chewies. Or, for something different, see if your pet likes alfalfa squares.

Although pet-store chews are the safest, you don't need to go the store-bought route for gnaw toys. If the budget is tight, coconut shells or empty Brazil-nut shells will keep your pet's teeth trimmed. If you have any trees in your backyard, your hamster might appreciate some all-natural chews. For example, leafy twigs and branches from apple, ash, aspen, beech, hickory, pear, and willow trees are safe for pets to chew on. If you have access to any other trees not listed here, check with your veterinarian first to find out if they're safe for pets . . . the wood and bark of some trees are toxic to animals. Also

make sure that any twigs you offer come from trees that have never been sprayed, and always rinse them well to get rid of any bugs. Although twigs from the backyard can be okay, wood from the home workshop is not. You can't be certain that wood picked up at the local lumber yard has never been treated with chemicals or preservatives.

One last word on gnawing. Gnawing is normal, but obsessive gnawing is not. Compulsive chewing has more to do with boredom than with keeping teeth trimmed. If your hamster can't stop chewing, especially on the cage bars, perhaps she needs a more expansive cage setup, more out-of-the-cage playtime, and more stimulating toys.

Chapter Seven
Potty Training

Why bother?

It's no secret that hamster urine has a strong odor. If you're cleaning out the cage only once a week, the smell can get pretty overwhelming between cage cleanings. What's more, the ammonia fumes that are produced as urine breaks down can irritate your hamster's respiratory membranes.

However, if you train your pet to confine his waste to a covered potty that can be emptied frequently, you'll go a long way toward reducing the fumes and the smell. You'll be happier. Your hamster will be happier. And the cage will be a more comfortable and healthy place for your pet. What better reasons to give potty training a try?

A natural instinct

Litter training a hamster is not usually difficult. Why? Because hamsters are clean animals whose natural habit is to urinate (but not always to defecate) in the same spot every time, usually in a cor-

ner. To litter-train your pet, you take advantage of this trait and place a hamster potty in the corner that he chooses as his bathroom.

The right equipment

Start by finding a suitable hamster potty. You're in luck here! Most pet shops that carry hamster supplies have inexpensive potties in stock. Some are triangular to fit nicely into a cage corner. Others are rectangular. All have hinged or removable tops and a hamster-sized opening in the front.

If you don't want to spend money buying a potty, you can eas-

ily make one for no cost at all. First, look for a small, sturdy plastic container with a lid. Next, make a 2- to 3-inch (5 to 7.5 cm) hole in one side of the container. Locate this hole about 1 inch (2.5 cm) above the base, or ½ inch (1 cm) for dwarf hamsters. Last, sand the edges smooth for safe entries and exits.

A plastic potty might have to be replaced from time to time if the plastic absorbs the urine odor or if your hamster shows any interest in gnawing the opening. Unfortunately, most plastic containers are not nibble-proof. So, rather than providing your pet with a plastic potty, you might want to give him a nonporous, gnaw-proof, glass potty instead.

The great thing about a glass litter box is that there are absolutely no do-it-yourself skills involved in setting one up. All you need to do is get hold of a 1-pint (500 ml), widemouthed canning jar with flat sides—or a square ½-pint (250 ml) glass jar for a dwarf hamster—pop it into a corner of the cage, and you have an instant hamster restroom. It's easy to clean, it can't be chewed, it won't roll like a round jar would, and it will last as long as your hamster does.

After the potty is chosen, litter is next on the list. Store-bought hamster toilets come complete with a little bag of litter and a scoop. Don't use this litter; it's clumping litter, and clumping litter can cause respiratory problems in small animals. Instead, just put a layer of whatever you're using as bedding into the potty (see Chapter 2). The great

advantage of having a hamster toilet is that cleanup is very easy. You just lift out the container and toss out its contents every day. Then wash it out and replace the litter. This is much easier than scooping out soiled bedding from a corner and then trying to wash out the corner without getting the rest of the bedding wet.

Getting down to business

You've chosen the potty and the litter . . . now it's your hamster's turn to make a choice. He has to pick out the location for his bathroom. Whatever corner gets his repeat business is the corner where the potty should be placed. Don't bother making the choice yourself without consulting your pet. He'll just ignore the corner you've chosen and go where he wants to go. Are you setting up a new cage? Be patient. Don't put the litter box into the cage until your hamster has christened a corner.

When the bathroom facilities are in place, toilet training can begin. Cover the bottom of the potty with a layer of litter (bedding), and add some urine-soaked bedding along with a few droppings. As soon as your hamster is wide awake, place him at the outhouse opening so that he can get a whiff of what's inside. This lets him know what that funny little house in the corner is

for. Then, when nature calls, his natural instinct should take over and prompt him to step right in and relieve himself.

Never, ever force your hamster into the potty. You don't want to turn him off the idea of toilet training. Instead, let him investigate the litter box at his own pace. Most hamsters eventually catch on.

Bedroom, bathroom, or kitchen?

Some hamsters are delighted with their new bathroom . . . but not for its intended purpose. They see it as a bedroom or a kitchen, and prefer to sleep in it or stash food

in it. What are the reasons for this? Usually a hamster sleeps in his litter pan because he hasn't been provided with separate sleeping quarters or because the sleep house he has been given isn't to his liking. Usually a hamster hoards food in the litter pan because his cage is too small for him to find alternative hiding places for the food. What can you do to get your pet to use his potty as a potty?

First, take a look at the cage. Is it big enough to accommodate a small litter box, exercise equipment, and at least one comfy sleep house, and still have room left over for several food stashes? If not, get a bigger cage or add more sections to the existing one. If the size of the cage isn't the problem, then take a look at the sleep house. Maybe it's not the right size. Maybe the nesting material is not to your hamster's liking? Reread Chapters 1 and 2 to review the information on cages, beds, and bedding.

The uncooperative hamster

Hamsters aren't always 100 percent cooperative about litter training. For example, your pet might decide that it's okay to urinate in the box but not to defecate in it. This is common, and there's not much you can do to change

this behavior. However, it's easy enough to get rid of the droppings between cage cleanings. Just pick them out with an old spoon or a pair of tweezers. And speaking of droppings, don't get upset if you notice your pet gobbling them down every so often. Hamsters practice coprophagy, which means they eat some of their soft feces to obtain residual vitamins and minerals. This isn't as gross as it sounds . . . it's just a hamster's way of recycling food to get the maximum nutritional value from it.

Another way a hamster can be uncooperative is to use more than one corner for bathroom breaks, especially if he's housed in a large or multi-section cage. Don't try

to confine him to a single corner. This could cause him undue stress. Instead, follow his lead, and put potties in each of his chosen corners. If you have two or more dwarf hamsters, you might need to provide each of them with a separate potty.

Although most hamsters are good candidates for litter training, there's always the odd renegade that doesn't get the hang of things. Be patient: often it's just a matter of time. However, if the box continues to be boycotted, don't force the issue. Rather than upsetting yourself and stressing your hamster, it's better to use highly absorbent bedding in the cage and resign yourself to daily corner cleaning.

57

Chapter Eight
Make the Cage a Hamster Heaven

Phys. Ed. . . . Your hamster needs a daily workout

Take a look at your small hamster with her short legs. Would you ever believe that in the wild she can cover miles in a single night? Now look at her cage. How much exercise can she get in that limited space? The fact is, your hamster is going to spend much of her life in her cage, and no matter how many tubes and modules you join together, you won't be able to give her miles of cage to explore. So what's the answer? Well, it's a combination of things. You have to give her as expansive a cage setup as possible (see Chapter 1). You have to give her as much out-of-the-cage playtime as possible (see Chapters 9 and 10). And, you have to give her toys, running wheels, climbers, and other play-

things to keep her physically fit and mentally alert.

The quality of your hamster's life is totally up to you. It's you who will have to make the cage a hamster health club . . . a fitness center and playground all rolled into one. In such a stimulating environment, your hamster will be able to follow her natural instincts and get the workout she needs. She'll be able to keep her body in shape and her

mind alive. In other words, she'll be happy. And a happy hamster is easy to handle and easy to train.

Running on a hamster wheel

How do you provide your pet with the marathon practice she needs? The easiest way is to let her loose on a hamster wheel. However, not all hamster wheels are created equal—you must be careful when making a choice. If you buy a wheel that has a running surface made of rungs or mesh, your hamster's fragile feet and legs could be injured or broken if they get caught in the spaces between the rungs or

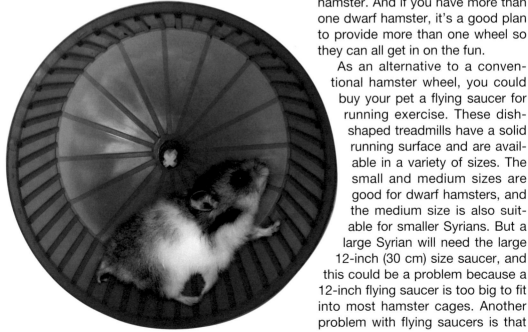

the mesh. For safety's sake, you should always buy a wheel that has a solid running surface and no cross bars. Some of these solid wheels are open on one side; others are enclosed but have several entrance holes. Some solid wheels are stand-alone; others attach to the cage.

Wheel size is all-important, too. A wheel that is too small can cause spinal damage by forcing your hamster to bow her back unnaturally as she runs. Don't buy a small hamster wheel for your baby Syrian. That baby will grow, but the wheel will not. A wheel for a Syrian should never be less than 8 inches (20 cm) in diameter, and bigger is better. A small wheel, 6.5 inches (16.5 cm) in diameter, will be fine for a dwarf hamster. And if you have more than one dwarf hamster, it's a good plan to provide more than one wheel so they can all get in on the fun.

As an alternative to a conventional hamster wheel, you could buy your pet a flying saucer for running exercise. These dish-shaped treadmills have a solid running surface and are available in a variety of sizes. The small and medium sizes are good for dwarf hamsters, and the medium size is also suitable for smaller Syrians. But a large Syrian will need the large 12-inch (30 cm) size saucer, and this could be a problem because a 12-inch flying saucer is too big to fit into most hamster cages. Another problem with flying saucers is that some hamsters run so fast, they fly right off. If this happens, they're at risk of being injured by colliding with the walls of the cage or with a cage accessory, like a sleep house. If your hamster keeps flying off her saucer, stick with a wheel.

Unfortunately, most hamster wheels and saucers are made of plastic. In fact, it's difficult to find any other kind. So what are your options if your pet is an obsessive plastic chewer? You could try smearing a little bitter gel on the chewed area. Or, you could search the Internet for a metal wheel or saucer that will be the right size for your pet and her cage. Another possibility would be to buy a plastic wheel that's made of really sturdy plastic (replace when necessary), or a brand that offers replacement parts.

One of the main points to consider when you're scouting out a wheel is the noise factor. Your hamster won't care how much racket she makes on her nightly marathons. But you might! Or your partner might, or the kids might, or your neighbors in the next apartment might. There's nothing more annoying at 3:00 A.M. than the rumble-rumble or the squeak-squeak of a noisy hamster wheel. Read the reviews on the Internet, or spin those wheels at the pet shop before making a choice. Are none of the pet-store wheels quiet? You might be able to fix a squeaky one at home with a few drops of vegetable oil. If this doesn't work, return it and surf the Net for one that's marketed as being "silent."

Often a cage comes with a wheel . . . and often this wheel isn't the greatest. Check it out. Is it too small, or does the running surface have rungs? Don't keep a substandard wheel just because it comes with the cage. For your hamster's sake, get rid of it and buy another model.

Whatever kind of wheel you buy, it's important to keep it clean. Any wheel with a solid running surface

is going to collect urine and feces. It's messy and unhygienic to let pee and poops sit on the running surface, so be sure to clean your hamster's wheel on a daily basis.

Because hamsters are such big fans of wheel running, some become obsessive and run to the point of exhaustion. If you find that your pet is jogging round and round nonstop, perhaps it's because she has nowhere else to run and nothing else to do. Take a good look at her cage setup. Is it too small and cramped? Then invest in a more extensive cage layout for added running room. Now take a look at her cage furniture. Does she have any other equipment to exercise on? Right from the start, a wheel should be just one exercise option among many (see the next section). One last thing to consider: Does your hamster get enough out-of-the-cage playtime? Running free in a supervised play area should be part of her daily routine.

Sometimes a bigger cage, more equipment, and extra out-of-the-cage playtime will make no difference to a hamster's compulsive running. In this case, let her run the wheel in the early evening, but take it out of the cage when you go to bed at night so that she has to explore other exercise options.

Banish boredom

Your pet is going to spend hours and hours and hours in her cage.

Don't let those hours be dull, boring ones. Instead, provide your hamster with many and varied activities to keep her on the move and keep her brain cells working. Toys, tunnels, seesaws, and climbers will all make your pet's life an interesting and active one. See Chapter 11 to find out more about the best store-bought and homemade hamster playthings.

Whatever equipment you decide to put into your pet's cage, make sure it can't tip over. A seesaw, a ramp, or a puzzle gym that's wobbling around on lumpy bedding is an accident waiting to happen. So, for safety's sake, check frequently that every toy is stable and firmly in place.

Rearranging the furniture . . . or not?

One way to keep your hamster on her toes is to rearrange her cage every so often . . . one item at a time, please, so she doesn't get stressed. You could take the seesaw out of one module and put it into a different module for a while. Or, you could reconfigure the tubes system that leads from the main cage to the burrowing box. Or, you could take an old toy out of the cage and replace it with a new one. The old toy can be recycled into the cage a few weeks later, when it will seem like a new toy again.

However, don't get carried away and rearrange *everything* in the cage at once. If you do, your hamster could get stressed out and possibly even sick. And don't upset your pet by moving her sleep house, potty, food dish, or water bottle. Hamsters are creatures of habit. When it comes to their basic living arrangements, they like a place for everything and everything in its place. So plan on moving only the fun stuff. After all, it's the fun stuff that's going to keep your hamster active and alert.

Keep in mind, too, that some hamsters won't tolerate having even their playthings moved around. These stubborn pets get upset and agitated by change of any kind. They like their cage contents and setup to remain the same yesterday, today, and tomorrow. Whenever you move anything in the cage, keep an eye on your hamster to make sure that the new arrangement is to her liking. If she becomes distressed or is unable to settle down, go back to the old familiar arrangement.

Chapter Nine

Out to the Playground for Recess

Is it possible? Is it practical?

In the last chapter, you learned how important exercise is for your hamster and how to provide workout opportunities for him in the cage. But why confine exercise to the cage? One of the very best ways to see that your pet gets a good aerobic workout is to let him have some supervised out-of-the-cage playtime. Of course, you can't let your hamster have free run of the house like a dog or a cat. Think of the safety issues. A small hamster could be stepped on and squashed; he could vanish without a trace into the walls, heating ducts, or appliances. Think, too, of the property damage he could do. You might not be able to see your hamster, but you will certainly see the path of destruction he leaves . . . gnawed woodwork, nibbled rugs, chewed upholstery.

So if you can't let your pet loose in the house, just how is he going to get out-of-the-cage exercise? The answer is a small, hamster-proofed room, or a pet playpen.

Hamster proofing

If you want to go the hamster-proofed room route, then you have to know what hamster proofing is. To put it briefly, hamster proofing is making the hamster's play space safe—safe *for* him, and safe *from* him. When you're choosing a play space, look at it from your hamster's point of view. Can he escape? Can he get hurt? Then look at it from your point of view. What can your pet nibble or gnaw? When you know what you're up against, you'll realize that your choice of possible play places is fairly limited.

The best bet is the bathroom

In most homes or apartments, the bathroom is the best place for a hamster playground. For a start, bathrooms usually have a door . . . better yet, a door that locks. A closed door will keep your pet in, and a locked door will keep other people out, making the bathroom a traffic-free zone. Most bathrooms are small, so they won't require much hamster proofing. There's not much furniture to be chewed, and the floor is usually washable.

The first and easiest step in hamster proofing is to clear the floor. Pick up anything that your pet could chew. Towels, bath rugs, clothes—anything chewable should be put away, and any towels that are dangling over the side of the tub need to be moved. Otherwise, if your hamster tries to climb the towel, both hamster and towel will come crashing down. Move any wicker wastebaskets that could be climbed, and make sure all electrical cords are out of reach.

Then take a look at the heating vent covers. Fancy grillwork covers could provide an open door into the heating system. Metal louvered types could trap, cut, or injure your

pet's delicate feet, so cover up those vents. A ceramic tile makes an ideal temporary cover, but a piece of heavy cardboard weighted down will work fine as well. Do you have baseboard heaters rather than floor vents? Unless the design is such that your hamster can't get burned and can't nibble at the wires, you should plan on using a pet playpen instead of a bathroom for your pet's out-of-the-cage play-time (see the last section in this chapter).

Now inspect the plumbing. If there are any gaps where the pipes go through the floor or into the wall, plug them up with wall-repair compound. Even a small gap needs immediate attention, because a dwarf hamster could squeeze right through, and a Syrian could soon gnaw at a small hole and make it a big hole. Make sure the sink vanity is flush against the wall. If there's a gap, nail up a piece of wooden molding to cover it . . . this will prevent your pet from escaping. Then check to see if there's a space between the kickboard and the cupboard that's big enough for your pet to crawl into. To fix a narrow space, nail up a piece of quarter-round molding. For larger openings, replace the kickboard with a taller one. Or, cut a piece of thin plywood or wafer board to fit, nail this in place, and cover it with the old kickboard.

While you're checking for spaces and gaps, take a look at the bathroom door. It doesn't take much

of a gap between the door and the floor for a hamster to crawl under. A draft stop, a door sweep, or an old jammed-in towel will keep your pet on the right side of the door.

Has your hamster started chewing the baseboards or the corners of the cabinets? If so, smear on some bitter gel (see Chapter 6). And if your bathroom doubles as a greenhouse, put all plants out of hamster reach, because the leaves of many common household plants are poisonous to animals.

Off-limits

In most homes, a bathroom is the most practical place for a hamster playground. However, if the bathroom's too busy in your house, there might be another room that could be used for a play place. What about a mudroom, an exercise room, or a sewing room?

As long as you can hamster-proof the room, it's a possibility. Do you have a hallway that can be closed off? That's another potential playground. Take a good look at your living space . . . only you can decide what area or areas can be made safe for your hamster.

Are there any places that should be totally off-limits? Living rooms, family rooms, and bedrooms are not usually practical playrooms. Why not? The flooring is not always suitable, there are too many places to hide, and there is too much wood to gnaw and too much upholstery to chew. In other words, too much trouble. Laundry rooms aren't practical either. Hamsters can creep under and into the washer and dryer. They can nibble the drive belts, and escape outside by chewing through the dryer vent. So unless you can completely block off the appliances, keep laundry rooms off-limits. The same goes for the kitchen. In addition

to the problem of completely hamster-proofing all of the appliances, there are also hygiene concerns.

Pet playpens

Perhaps your house is too old to lend itself to hamster proofing, perhaps it's too elegant, or perhaps you don't have the time. Does this mean that your hamster can't get out of the cage to play? No. There is another option. You could invest in a pet playpen. In fact, for dwarf hamsters that are so small and

quick, a pet playpen is your best option for out-of-the-cage playtime.

However, not just any pet playpen will do. Some owners buy small-pet playpens made of connectable wire panels. But there's a potential problem with these pens: many Syrians and dwarfs are expert at scaling the bars and climbing out. And once your hamster has figured out how to do this, the playpen is useless! So instead of a wire-panel system, you might want to invest in a pet playpen that is actually a roll of stiff but flexible plastic that unrolls and stands on edge to form a large enclosure. It's available in a 10-inch-high (25 cm) size or a 24-inch-high (60 cm) size. Which size should you buy? It depends. A hamster can't climb the smooth plastic wall, so the 10-inch one would do as long as your hamster can't climb up a toy and get over it. If you're unsure, buy the taller size. Set the playpen on a washable floor for easy cleanup, or if you're limited to carpeted areas, lay down a shower curtain before unrolling the playpen.

Are you short on cash? Why not make your own pet corral? First, get some sturdy cardboard boxes, at least a foot high (30 cm). Next, remove the top and bottom flaps. Now slice through one of the corner crease lines on each box so that the cardboard can be opened out flat. Then, tape the boxes together to form a pet playpen. This homemade playpen has many advantages. Its size can be customized by adding or subtracting boxes, it folds flat for storage, and when it gets worn, you can make a new one.

For an instant playpen that doesn't require any time or money, there's always the empty bathtub. Just plug up the drain hole, and cover the slippery bottom with a couple of bathmats or with a cheap, flannel-backed, vinyl tablecloth. (No terry-cloth towels, please . . . hamsters can get their claws caught in the loops.) You should also drape the shower curtain to the outside of the tub in case your pets try to climb it or use it as an escape route.

Warning! Whether you go the store-bought, the homemade, or the instant route, it's very important to remember that a pet playpen is NOT a pet-sitting service. Hamsters should NEVER be left unsupervised in a pet playpen.

Chapter Ten

Practice Sessions in the Play Place

Step-by-step instructions

The play place is picked out and hamster proofed. Now the question is: Have you and your hamster bonded yet? Don't introduce your hamster to the world beyond the cage until you're completely comfortable with each other. This is important. If your pet is jittery around you, leaving the security of her cage could be stressful. And if you're jittery around your pet, you could drop her.

When it's time to get your pet out of the cage for the first time, do it in the evening. That's when, in their natural habitat, hamsters come out of their burrows to forage; that's when they're awake and ready to go. Before getting started, make sure you have some food and water, a potty, some toys, and a sleep house in the play area . . . all of this will help your hamster feel at home.

For safe transport from the cage to the play place, there are a few options. First, you could pick up your pet and cup her against your chest. Do this only if your hamster is completely comfortable with being held. Second, you could encourage your pet to go into a tube in the cage, and then pick up the tube, covering the ends with your hands, and carry it over to the play area. Third, you could put a tiny treat into a family-sized yogurt container and wait for your pet to go inside for the treat. Then, resting the lid loosely over the top, carry the container and its contents over to the playground.

Let your hamster explore the new area at her own pace. Don't go grabbing at her, putting her here and putting her there, trying to make her play with the toys. What you can do, however, is set out some treats and some nesting material that she can forage for. This gives some point to her explorations, and mimics what she'd be doing in the wild.

In the beginning, keep out-of-the-cage time short—perhaps 10 minutes—but provide it daily so that your hamster gets used to it. When she's obviously enjoying her-

self, gradually extend her playtime until you've worked up to half an hour or so of free roaming . . . or whatever period of time you and your hamster are comfortable with.

Never make loud noises or sudden movements when your pet is out playing. And, keep the kids under control. Don't let them chase at, grab at, poke at, or yell at their new pet. After all, stressing out your hamster isn't the goal of playtime.

Always supervise

NEVER let your hamster run around in the play place unsupervised. No matter how confident you are about your hamster-proofing skills, there's no telling what your pet could get into or chew through when your back's turned. Do you want to return to the bathroom and find a corner of the baseboard chewed? Of course not! So if the doorbell rings, don't leave your hamster running around unsupervised. Pick her up and put her back into the cage.

You might think it's okay to leave your hamster alone in a pet playpen. But think again. Many a hamster has found a way to escape from a playpen.

Do's and don'ts

The following do's and don'ts will help keep your hamster safe and stress-free when she's in her playground.

• Do let your pet out to play in the evening when she's awake and alert. Remember, waking a hamster causes it stress.

- Do exercise crowd control. With too many people in the play area, an accident is more likely to happen.
- Do keep the bathroom locked when you're using it as a playroom. This prevents people from coming in unexpectedly and possibly hitting your hamster with the door. It also prevents your hamster from escaping when the door is opened.
- Do get into the habit of sitting down during playtime. If you're not standing up, you can't step on your hamster.
- Don't wear shoes. Wear socks and shuffle your feet along the floor rather than stepping normally. After all, you can't step on your hamster if you don't take any steps.
- Don't treat your hamster as a toy. She's a living, breathing creature, and not a stuffed animal. Always handle her gently.

Clean up the accidents

Will your hamster use the potty you provided in the play area? Maybe yes; maybe no. But even if she does use it regularly, accidents will happen. Fortunately, hamsters don't make much of a mess. And if you've chosen the playground wisely, the floor will be easy to clean. Just wipe up any accidents with a paper towel, and give the floor a quick mop with a pet sanitizer when playtime is over.

Catching that hamster

Playtime's over! It's time for your pet to go back into her cage. But your pet has other ideas. She wants a longer playtime, and keeps running away when you try to catch her. Now what? Whatever you do, don't chase her—you'll only frighten her. You could try calling your pet by using the knock or whistle technique you learned in Chapter 5. Or, you could put a favorite treat onto the palm of your hand. Then when your pet climbs onto your hand to get it, cup your other hand around her and carry her off to the cage. Another strategy is to place a tunnel/tube or glass jar on the floor with a treat in it. Then when your hamster walks inside the tube, cup a hand over the end(s), and carry her back to the cage.

Chapter Eleven
Fun Time

Off to the store or onto the Internet

Do you want to keep your pet active? Do you want to make sure he's never bored? Do you want to create—even in a small way—the opportunity for physical and mental stimulation that wild hamsters get on their nightly foraging expeditions? Then fun activities, both in the cage and in the play area, are a must for your pet.

A quick trip to your local pet store, or a quick browse on the Internet, will turn up a wide selection of toys and fun stuff that your hamster can climb on and crawl through. Many hamster toys are made of plastic, but if your hamster is a compulsive plastic-chewer, try to find wooden or grass toys instead. What's available in natural materials? Look for wooden tunnels and barrels, wooden seesaws and bridges, grass and bamboo balls, and willow tunnels and balls, as well as wooden swings and playgrounds. Now the question is: With so much choice in hamster toys, how do you know what will appeal

to your hamster? Unfortunately, you can't tell in advance which items your pet will go for and which ones he'll ignore. But, fortunately, hamster toys aren't usually expensive, so any rejected toys won't be a huge waste of money. (Why not donate them to your local animal shelter?)

Even the best playthings can become boring with overuse, so to give your hamster some variety in his life, introduce new toys from time to time. You could also remove familiar toys and reintroduce them at a later date, or combine and recombine old toys in new ways . . . anything to keep the environment stimulating and challenging. And remember, always check play stuff regularly for wear and tear, and throw out anything that's too chewed up to be safe.

Tubes, tunnels, and mazes

You can't provide too many tubes and tunnels for your hamster. After all, in the wild, hamsters

new configurations every so often.

If your hamster is an obsessive plastic-chewer, you could try using sections of PVC pipe and PVC connectors instead. PVC is much harder than the made-for-hamster plastic tunnels, and withstands your hamster's gnawing much better. PVC piping comes in a variety of different diameters, so you can customize a system for either dwarf hamsters or a Syrian.

Store-bought mazes also give your pet room to roam in a limited space. Just be sure to secure the lid of the maze to the maze itself by taping it down tightly or by securing the top to the bottom with a tight-fitting rubber band or a long shoestring. Otherwise, your hamster could pop off the lid and pop out.

No matter which plastic tubes, tunnels, and/or mazes you buy, you'll have to clean them regularly, because hamsters pee and poop as they run through the tunnels and mazes. In the cage, your pet's waste is absorbed by the bedding. But in the tubes, the waste sits on the plastic and causes a buildup of ammonia and a strong odor. To keep your pet healthy, tunnels should be cleaned once or twice a week. It's a time-consuming job to take a tunnel system apart, wash it thoroughly, rinse it, dry it, and put it back together again. So take this into consideration before you go overboard on the tunnels!

If you want to provide a tunnel system made of natural materials

spend their days hiding and sleeping in a network of underground tunnels. You can provide this same experience for your pet by setting up a network of tunnels and tubes in the cage and/or the play area. Connect straight or curved plastic hamster tubes to elbows, U-turns, and Ts, for a challenging labyrinth. Fortunately, you don't have to buy everything at once . . . you can build it up a piece at a time. And to keep your hamster interested, you can recombine the sections into for your pet, then your choices are more limited. You'll have to opt for short sections of wood, grass, or pet-quality cardboard. However, you won't be able to join these together, and they'll be difficult (or impossible) to clean.

Up, up, up!

Hamsters have strong legs for their small size. This muscular strength makes them natural climbers. So give your pet something to climb on. Small wooden ramps and bridges, hamster gyms and playgrounds, and hamster playhouses all give your pet an opportunity to climb safely.

Safety is a real issue for a climbing hamster. It's not so much the getting up that's the problem—it's the coming down. Although hamsters are surefooted on the way up, they're not so well coordinated when it comes to getting down. In fact, a hamster will often intentionally drop from a height rather than climb down. This isn't too much of a problem in a wild hamster's natural habitat where a falling hamster would have a soft, sandy landing. But in the cage or in the play area, a pet that falls or drops from a height is liable to have a serious crash landing. A broken leg, pelvis, or spine is not uncommon for hamsters that fall, even from modest heights. So the number one rule when picking a climbing apparatus for your pet is to make sure the climbers are low.

If your hamster does fall from a height, and shows any signs of limping, dragging a limb, hiding, or acting oddly, don't take a wait-and-see attitude. Take him to a veterinarian immediately and have him checked over.

Down, down, down!

Hamsters are not only agile climbers, but also expert diggers. So, here's an opportunity to provide your pet with some digging activities he'll really enjoy. The first activity gives your hamster a chance to burrow. To get him started, invest in a burrowing module for the cage setup, or buy a small add-on cage module that can be turned into a burrowing tank by filling it with soft bedding. It won't take your pet long to figure out what the new module is for!

The second activity involves giving your pet his own sandbox in the play area. Buy a cheap plastic storage box and a bag of play sand. Pour some sand into the box, plunk in your pet, and watch him start digging! A few buried sunflower seeds will turn the digging expedition into a treasure hunt.

As a third activity, many hamsters enjoy taking sand baths. Any small container will do, or you can buy a ceramic chinchilla or critter bath. Pour in some dust-free chinchilla sand, then sit back and watch the fun. (Never use chinchilla dust; it's not good for your hamster's respiratory system.)

Seesaw antics

Most hamsters are big teeter-totter fans, whether they're going up and down on a wooden seesaw, or in and out of the plastic-tube kind. Of course, this is a solo activity for your pet . . . there won't be a hamster at each end. What a hamster does is run up one side of the seesaw and down the other — again, and again, and again. Some hamsters catch on to this pastime without help. But if your hamster doesn't, here's what to do. Take small pieces of his favorite treat and line them up the middle of the seesaw. Then as your pet walks up the seesaw to get the treats, his weight will tip the balance and he'll get the feel for how the teeter-totter works. Repeat the treat line daily until your hamster uses the toy without a treat reward.

Homemade toys

Is there anything around the house suitable for a hamster toy? Try crumpling up some plain,

unused white paper—computer paper, facial tissues, or tissue paper are all okay. What about a paper-towel tube or a toilet-paper tube or an empty tissue box? Do these make good hamster play-things? Not really. Cardboard tubes and boxes often contain glues that are toxic to hamsters. Toss the tubes and give them a few unbleached paper towels or tissues instead.

For more homemade hamster toys, why not raid your kitchen cupboards? Food-grade paper cups turned on their sides make great pet caves. If you place a few of these around the cage or play place, your pet can run in and out of them, drag bedding into them, and even curl up in them for a snooze.

Another easy-to-make toy is a paper-bowl hidey-hole. There's not much involved in making one of these. Just turn a food-grade paper bowl upside down, cut out an entrance hole in the side, and stuff the bowl with tissues. You can make these hidey holes out of food-safe, plant-fiber bowls, too.

How about making a pet play box? All that's needed is a small, sturdy cardboard box (the folded kind without glue) and a pair of scissors. Cut out a few hamster-sized holes in the box, and that's all there is to it! To make a bun-ker instead, cut two holes in the top of the box and bury the box in the cage bedding so that only the holes are visible. Now your pet has an underground den whenever he wants to hide.

Small, clay flowerpots are another hamster favorite. Turned upside down, they're climbers; turned on their side, they're caves.

Chapter Twelve
Roll-Around Balls

An easy answer to the exercise question

Is your house impossible to hamster-proof? Does your pet need more room to exercise than a play-pen can provide? Then a hamster ball might just solve the problem of how your pet is going to get a good workout.

Rodent on a roll

By now you know that to stay healthy, hamsters need exercise . . . and plenty of it! You also know that they can become compulsive wheel runners if their aerobic options are limited. Your goal should be to provide different types of exercise for your pet so that she doesn't become obsessed with any one activity. With this in mind, why not get your pet a roll-around ball? This is an exercise option that many hamsters enjoy.

These balls come in several different styles. Most common are the everyday, free-roll balls. You'll also find some that roll on a track, some that come with stands, and some that look like race cars or princess coaches. They come in different sizes, too, and it's very important to pick a size that suits your pet. Mini-balls are strictly for dwarf hamsters. Never put a Syrian into one of these; her back will be bent unnaturally. And never put a dwarf hamster into a large ball; as the ball turns, the dwarf hamster will be thrown around inside. If you have several brands to choose from at the store, opt for the one that has the most ventilation holes.

How does a roll-around ball work? You put your hamster inside the hollow plastic sphere and close the door securely, and when your pet starts running, the ball starts rolling. Most hamsters enjoy taking a whirl in a ball, and some hamsters become such expert navigators that they can maneuver it exactly where they want it to go. If you have one of these skillful drivers, you can set up a miniature obstacle course.

One of the great advantages of this exercise equipment is that your pet's playtime won't be limited

to a small room any longer. She'll be able to explore non-hamster-proofed rooms in the safety of an enclosed plastic sphere. But if you don't want your pet rolling around your house at will, why not invest

in a hamster track? A hamster rolling on a track will be able to cover a lot of ground without rolling out of sight.

"Gimme a break!"

No matter how much your pet enjoys touring around the house or on a track in her own hamster transport, don't let her ride to the point of exhaustion—too much running and she could become overheated and/or dehydrated. Keep in mind, too, that although a hamster can get out of an exercise wheel when she needs a drink or a rest, she's stuck in that ball until you let her out. It's up to you to monitor her ball rolling and see that she's never put into the ball and forgotten.

How long should you let your hamster run in a ball? You should give your pet a break every 10 to 15 minutes. Take her out of the ball and put her back in the cage so she has a chance to rest, take a drink, and use the potty.

Caution: hamster at play!

To make sure your hamster can exercise safely in the ball, here are some important rules:

• After putting your pet into the ball, latch the door properly to prevent escape or injury.

• Keep the ball on the floor. Never put it on a raised surface like a table; even a short fall could have fatal consequences.

• Block off any steps or stairs that the ball could bounce down.

• Keep other pets well away from the ball.

• Never let anyone push or kick the ball. Your hamster is the one who has to start the ball rolling.

• Supervise, supervise, supervise.

• Always clean the ball thoroughly after use . . . pee and poop can get trapped inside.

Not a hamster favorite?

When you introduce your pet to this exercise activity, stick to the tried-and-true training techniques . . . start with short sessions and

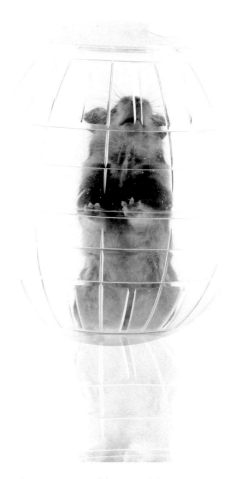

work up to longer ones. You could start with a 2-minute ride and gradually work up to a 10-minute session. Always watch for your pet's reaction. If she's obviously enjoying herself, let her have fun. If she's frightened or doesn't want to get into the ball, forget the whole idea. It's not worth having a stressed-out hamster.

Chapter Thirteen

A Simple Training Technique — Lure-Reward Training

Follow the food

As soon as your hamster (Syrian) or hamsters (dwarfs) feel at home and feel comfortable with you, it's time to get down to some fun training. You'll be amazed at the number of behaviors and tricks a hamster can perform. So, let's get started! In the next couple of chapters, you'll read about the two main techniques for training your pet(s). The first and simplest technique is known as lure-reward training, and it involves a four-step process:

1. Give your hamster a verbal cue, such as "Up!"
2. Entice your pet to perform the desired behavior by luring him with a treat.
3. Your hamster performs the behavior.
4. You reward him with the treat.

This technique is most successful if you schedule sessions when your hamster is hungry. After all, your pet won't be too interested in treats if he has just gobbled down a big meal. Also, it's important in lure-reward training to find the *right* treat.

What is the right treat?

When picking a treat for lure-reward training, there are two points to keep in mind. First, you need to find a healthful treat that your hamster truly enjoys and is eager to follow. This might not be the same treat for every hamster. (See "The trick is in the treat" in Chapter 5). Second, it's best to lure your pet with a good-sized treat like a sprig of parsley, a blade of wheat grass, a slice of apple, or a slice of cucumber. Why? It's easy for your hamster to follow a sizable treat, and it's easy for you to let him have small nibbles as rewards. This is a lot simpler than constantly having to grab single, tiny pieces of cut-up food for lures.

The training location

The cage is not a great place to train a hamster. It's difficult to squeeze your hand into a cage, and there's not much space for luring. Not only that, but there are too many distractions in the cage. Your hamster isn't going to pay much attention to you when he has toys and tunnels to play with.

It's best to train hamsters in the play area (see Chapter 9), and it's best to train them one at a time. Of course, if you have a Syrian, this won't be an issue because they're loners anyway. But if you have a group of dwarf hamsters, pick out one trainee, and leave the others in the cage so they won't distract your pupil or compete for the treats. Don't start any training until your

hamster knows his way around the play area. And before each session, let your pet run around for a while to burn off his excess energy.

Standing up

With lure-reward training, it's very easy to get your hamster to stand up on his hind legs and beg. Before getting started, you'll need to pick up the toys in the play area so that your pet can focus on the job at hand. Then all you need is a little patience and the treats.

To start this lesson, sit on the floor and put your hamster down in front of you. Hold a treat, such as a parsley sprig, in front of his nose and let him sniff it. Then, when you've got your pet's attention, say "Up" or use a hand signal to indicate *up*. At the same time, start raising the parsley. Keeping it just out of your pet's reach, lure your hamster up until he's standing on his hind legs. Then let him take a bite as a reward.

Most hamsters are pretty agile and can be lured into a standing position at the first try. Then it's just a matter of practice and repetition: this is what ingrains the behavior and gets your hamster to connect the command with the standing. How long will this take? It's hard to say . . . it all depends on the individual hamster. Some hamsters can learn to stand on command fairly quickly. Others might take weeks of daily practice. Still others might never realize that "Up" means getting up on those hind legs. If your pet falls into this last category, then you'll always have to lure him with a treat. And that's okay, too.

A word of caution here: Not all hamsters are physically capable of standing up on their hind legs. Older hamsters, or those that are ill or have had injuries, might not be strong enough to perform this trick. Never push any hamster beyond its abilities! Training should be fun and safe.

Tackling a maze

One of the most fun things to teach a hamster is how to run a maze. But first, you'll have to buy or make one. It isn't difficult to design and build a maze yourself, or you can go on the Internet and see what other people have come up with. Mazes can be made out of wood, sturdy cardboard, foam board, or interlocking blocks. Whatever material you choose, make sure that the walls are either secured to a base or are sturdy enough so that they won't topple over onto your hamster. On the Internet you'll see some mazes made from books, DVD boxes, and/or old video boxes, but these are too unstable to be safe for your pet.

When you're designing a maze, draw a diagram first, and don't forget to include dead ends . . . a maze should be a challenge for your hamster.

There are three ways to teach your hamster how to navigate a maze, even a complex one. The first way is to lure your pet through. Begin by attracting his attention with a slice of apple. Now lead him along the correct path, encouraging him with a nibble of apple from time to time, and then giving him a bite of apple when he reaches the end. Repeat this training a few times. Then put him at the starting point and see if he can remember the right route. If he comes up against a dead end, wait for a moment or two to see if he can figure things out. If not, lure him through with the apple a few more times until he learns the correct route.

The second way of enticing your hamster through a maze is to lay a trail of tiny treats for your pet to follow. Start by cutting up a slice of cucumber into *very* small bits . . . believe it or not, you can get forty to fifty pieces out of one slice! Then, place single bits of cucumber along the correct path, spacing them 6 to 12 inches (15 to 30 cm) apart. Now put your hamster at the start of the maze and watch him gobble up the treats as he winds his way to the finish point. Repeat this step a couple of times to ingrain the route. That's enough for the first day's lesson, because you don't want your hamster gorging on too much cucumber. Over the next week or two, space the cucumber pieces farther and farther apart until eventually, there's only one small piece at the end of the route. By then, your pet should be scampering through the maze like a pro.

The third way for your hamster to find his way through a maze is by figuring things out for himself. This involves trial and error rather than training, but you do help your hamster by placing a reward at the end of the maze. After all, if he knows he's going to get a reward at the finish line, he'll try really hard to find the right way through.

You can have lots of fun with mazes. For example, if you have several dwarf hamsters, you can hold competitions. Buy a stopwatch, and keep track of how long it takes each one to learn the way through. When your hamster has mastered one maze layout, you can always challenge him with another.

Running an obstacle/agility course

Do you have an active and energetic Syrian, or some really rambunctious dwarf hamsters? If so, why not make a mini–obstacle/agility course and train your mini-athletes to race around it? An obstacle course is a fun way for your hamsters to keep fit and healthy, and a great way for you to interact with your pet(s).

Before you can train your hamster to run an agility course, you'll have to make the course. Here are some ideas for different obstacles you can make or buy.

• Build fences or hurdles from craft sticks or wooden stir sticks. For indi-

vidual hurdles, lay two craft sticks flat on a table, leaving a 3-inch (8 cm) space between them. Next, use a glue gun to attach two, three, or four crossbeams to the uprights. Be sure to leave a ¾-inch space (2 cm) at the bottom of each post, because the posts are going to be set into a modeling-clay or play-dough base. Now, lift up the hurdle, and stick each upright into a small lump of modeling clay. Wait for the clay to dry hard, and then glue the bases to a piece of corrugated cardboard, foam board, or smooth wood slat (found in craft stores). Securing the bases to a board prevents the hurdle from being knocked over by your hamster.

• Use heavy cardboard, foam board, or Coroplast to fashion a sturdy hurdle that consists of two side supports with a crossbeam slotted between them. Just make sure that any hurdles you make aren't too high . . . hamsters have short legs.

• Buy a small, barbell-shaped hand weight to use as a low hurdle.

• Use a bunch of craft sticks to build a really challenging combination obstacle that includes a series of hurdles and bars to jump over and run under (see photo).

• Secure a large, 3-inch (8 cm) plastic macramé ring or bird-toy ring, or a canning-jar ring, to two upright wooden dowels or craft sticks to make a hoop jump. Then, anchor the uprights in modeling clay, and glue the modeling

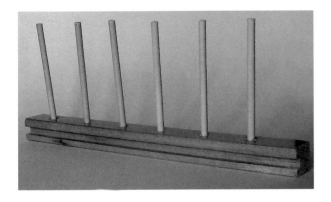

clay bases to a rectangular piece of foam board, heavy cardboard, wood slat, or Coroplast.

• Cut several rings from a foam can cooler. Then make a support frame by gluing two pieces of wooden dowel, 3¼ inches high (8.25 cm), to either end of a wood slat. These will be the end posts. Next, put the foam rings on a long dowel, and glue that dowel to the tops of the end posts. Lastly, position the rings evenly across the horizontal dowel, and use a glue gun to glue them in place. This makes a multi-hoop jump (see photo).

• Take a 1-inch by 1-inch (2.5 cm by 2.5 cm) strip of wood, approximately 12 inches (30 cm) long. Drill

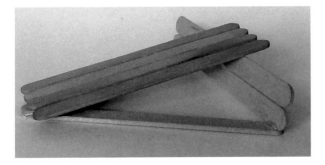

holes in it, and jam in or glue in short sections of wooden dowel to make a series of weave poles (see photo).

• Buy some hamster tunnels or sections of PVC pipe.

• Set up a hamster swing and/or a seesaw.

• Add a ramp or two. You can buy these, or you can make them out of craft sticks and/or craft-quality wood slats.

When you've finished putting the course together, grab a tasty treat, and set your hamster at the start line. Now what you're going to do is lure your pet over the course, one obstacle at a time. For example, if you're starting with a hurdle, give the command "Run," and lure your pet over the first jump. Then give him a treat, and repeat the hurdle training several times.

When he's mastered this first hurdle, it's time to move on to the next obstacle. If this obstacle is the combination jump, you'll have to give your pet the command "Run," get him to go over the first hurdle, then lure him over and under the various sections of the combination jump before giving him the treat. Repeat this sequence several times.

The idea is to train your hamster one obstacle at a time, until he has mastered the whole course. One way to do this is by starting with the first obstacle and working toward the last one. This is known as *forward chaining*. Another way to teach your hamster is by starting with the last obstacle, and working backward to the first one. This is known as *backward chaining*, a technique that can be very effective when the obstacle course is complex. If you have more than one hamster, it might be fun to try forward chaining with one and backward chaining with the other.

Some hamsters learn to run an obstacle course fairly quickly; others take longer to get the hang of things. A lot depends on the complexity of the course. Don't be surprised if it takes your hamster a month or more to learn a really complicated course. The species and ability level of the individual hamster makes a difference, too. For example, dwarf hamsters are particularly skilled at leaping over hurdles and negotiating obstacles. Syrians, on the other hand, are slower, and often plod around the course rather than sprint around it.

Whatever type of hamster you have, it's important never to push him beyond his capabilities. The whole idea is to provide mental stimulation and physical exercise for your pet . . . not to stress him out or exhaust him.

Random rewards

While your hamster is learning a behavior, it's important to hand out a reward each and every time he performs the behavior successfully. However, once he's mastered the trick, you could try cutting back on the treats a bit. Instead of rewarding your pet every single time he gets things right, try giving him a tidbit every second or third time. This is known as *intermittent reward*. Research shows that once a behavior is learned, intermittent rewards do a better job of reinforcing the behavior than giving a reward every single time.

A positive experience

Training should always be a positive experience, both for you and your pet. Learning should be fun. Never shout at or get upset with your hamster; he won't understand anyway. And if you find yourself getting frustrated because your pet isn't interested or isn't catching on fast enough, stop the session and try again later. It's always better to quit while you're ahead!

Chapter Fourteen

Click-Treat . . . The Clicker Training Technique

Clicking for success

In the previous chapter you learned how to teach your hamster some interesting activities by luring her with a treat. How did that go? Did she catch on pretty quickly? Did you both have fun? Now why not switch gears and try something different? In this chapter, you're going to learn how to train your pet by using a clicker. Clicker training, known as CT, is now one of the most popular and effective methods of training pets. You've probably heard of this technique being used with dogs, but what you might not know is that it can be used to train lots of other animals. For example, birds, cats, dolphins, ferrets, horses, rabbits, rats, and whales can all be trained with this technique. So why not give it a try with your hamster? To get started, all you need is a clicker and a supply of your hamster's favorite treats.

Picking a clicker and treats

A clicker is a small, handheld gadget that makes a *click* sound when it's pressed. They don't cost much, they come in different shapes and sizes, and you can find them in any pet store and on the Internet. Since they're small and easy to misplace, you should probably buy a couple of them at the same time so you can always get your hands on one when you need it. Be sure to buy the same type and brand so the clickers sound the same. Anything different could confuse your pet.

Some clickers have a louder click than others. For training a hamster, what you want is a clicker with a gentle click that won't frighten your pet. If you buy one from the Internet, and the sound scares your hamster, you could muffle the sound by wrapping the body of the clicker (but not the button) with electrical tape. Or, instead of buying a clicker, you could use a ballpoint pen, which has a quieter click. If you buy a ballpoint pen, don't be tempted to use it for writing; keep it strictly for training your pets. Otherwise, they'll get confused and think you're clicking for them.

What about the treats? Stick with the healthful ones (see Chapter 2 and Chapter 5), and cut them up into tiny pieces. This is important, because you'll be handing out quite a few treats in a training session, and you don't want to go over your pet's daily treat limit. Having trouble managing those tiny treats? You might find it easier to hold out a sprig of parsley and let your hamster take a small bite as a reward. Or you could put some plain yogurt into an eyedropper and reward your trainee with a drop at a time.

You shouldn't starve your pet before starting a training session, but it's a good idea to remove the food bowl about 60 minutes beforehand. This will ensure that your hamster doesn't have a full stomach and will be interested in those treats.

Charging the clicker

As with lure-reward training, it's best to start clicker training in the play area and to clear the area of all toys. Remember, too, that if you have more than one hamster, you'll need to train them one pet at a time. Ideally, the other hamsters shouldn't be able to hear the clicker, or they'll be expecting treats, too! Once you've picked your trainee, let her run off some of her energy so she'll be ready to pay attention to you.

Now, get down on the floor beside your pet. Press the clicker once, and immediately give your hamster a treat. Then, *click*-treat again. And again. And again. The only lesson you're trying to get across to your pet at this point is that a click equals a treat. This step is known as "loading" or "charging" the clicker. Timing is very important here. As soon as you click, give your hamster a reward.

To teach your pet that a click means a reward, you should click-treat several times in quick succession. That's enough for the first training session. Repeat the loading of the clicker a few times a day until your pet has made the connection between the click and the reward. How will you know when she's made the connection? Watch her behavior. When she looks for a reward as soon as she hears the clicker, you'll know she's made the link.

Teaching a behavior . . . touching a target stick

As soon as your pet realizes that a click gets her a treat, you can start teaching her specific behaviors. One

of the simplest behaviors to teach a hamster is how to touch, and then follow, a target stick.

You can buy one of these sticks at a pet store or on the Internet, but don't bother looking for one that's made specifically for use with hamsters. There are none! What you will find are target sticks for training dogs and cats. Many of these sticks are retractable; some even have a built-in clicker. This combo makes a lot of sense, because with the stick and clicker together in one hand, you'll have the other hand free for dispensing treats.

If you feel confident about managing a stick, a separate clicker, and the treats, you can make a target stick very cheaply. Buy a small sponge ball at a dollar store and jam it on to the end of a pencil, or on to a similar-sized piece of wooden dowel.

As soon as you have the target stick, you can start teaching your hamster how to touch it. Here are the steps involved. First, sit down in the play area, and position the ball of the target stick (or the tip of the stick if it doesn't have a ball) a couple of inches in front of your hamster's nose. Whenever your pet even *looks* at the tip of the stick, press the clicker and hand out a treat. Then repeat, repeat, repeat. Keep practicing this step over the next few days until your hamster is reliably looking at the stick in hopes of getting a treat. The next step is to hold the stick in the same position, but this time wait until your pet takes a step toward the target before clicking, treating, and repeating. Is this going well? Now wait until your hamster actually *touches* the stick before you click and treat. Once you get to this point, you click and treat only when your pet makes contact with the stick.

This whole step-by-step process is known as *shaping a behavior*. What you're actually doing is breaking up the behavior into small steps, and clicking/rewarding each step of the way. Do you have a really smart hamster? Then she might learn how to touch the stick pretty quickly. Is your hamster a slow learner? Then she might need several days (or weeks) of practice before she catches on.

When your hamster is reliably touching the stick, it's time to continue shaping her behavior so that she learns to touch the target stick when you hold it in a variety of different positions. For example, try holding the stick above your pet's nose. Then, as soon as she actually reaches up and touches the stick, click and treat. Repeat this step until your hamster is consistently touching the stick whenever you hold it up at this height. Next, hold the stick to the left of your hamster. When she's learned to touch it consistently on that side, teach her how to touch the stick when you move it to her right side. Keep in mind that your pet has to master one position before you start teaching her another.

Adding a cue

Has your hamster got the hang of touching a target stick? If so, it's time to add a command—known in clicker training as the *cue*. It might seem a bit strange to wait until your pet is reliably performing a behavior before adding a cue, but that's how it's done in clicker training. First, you ingrain the behavior by clicking and treating. Then, when your pet is doing exactly what you want, you add the cue. So how does this

work in target-stick training? You wait until your hamster has learned to touch the stick in a variety of positions. Only then do you add the command "Touch." Don't get carried away and say, "Touch, touch, touch." If you keep repeating the cue over and over, your hamster will think that "Touch, touch, touch" is the command, and won't respond if you say "Touch" just once.

Adding the cue is a process. In target-stick training, you start out by calling out "Touch" when your hamster's nose is right on the target (repeat, repeat). Then, change your timing so that you say "Touch" immediately before your hamster touches the target (repeat, repeat). Change your timing again, and call out the command as your pet is moving toward the target (repeat, repeat). What you're doing here is teaching your hamster to connect the command to the action. Your goal is to get to the point where your hamster will come right up to the stick and touch it whenever you say "Touch." When your hamster has learned to do this consistently, you can phase out the clicker for this behavior and start using it to teach something else.

Following a target stick

Now that your hamster is touching a target stick on command, the next step is to make that stick a moving target. Here's how. Hold the stick right in front of your hamster's nose, but don't let her touch it yet! Instead, start pulling the stick toward you. Your pet will probably follow it because she already knows that touching the target gets her a treat. After you've pulled the stick toward you about 6 inches (15 cm), let your hamster touch the target, and then click and treat. Repeat at this distance several times. That's enough for the first day's practice. In the next session, increase the distance to 8 inches (20 cm). Again click, treat, and repeat. Over the next few days, increase the distance in small increments, clicking, treating, and repeating each step of the way. Before you know it, your hamster will be following the stick across or around the play area! Then, add the "Follow" command the same way you added the "Touch" command in the last section.

When your hamster has learned to follow a target stick, you can use the stick to teach her other tricks or behaviors such as running through a tunnel, hopping through a hoop, or navigating an obstacle course. Just get your hamster to follow the moving stick.

Dispensing with the clicker

When your pet is successfully performing a behavior on cue, it's time to stop using the clicker to mark *that* behavior and start using it to teach a new behavior. In clicker training, the clicker is reserved for teaching new behaviors or for reteaching a skill that your hamster has forgotten.

And what about the rewards? Do you dispense with these, too? Not if you want your pet to keep performing! Even when you've stopped using the clicker for *training* a specific behavior, you'll still have to hand out treats for *rewarding* the completed behavior. If you don't, your pet will stop cooperating. However, as you learned in the lure-reward chapter, intermittent rewards often reinforce a behavior better than giving a reward every single time. Try giving rewards on a more random basis, and see how that works.

Keep clicking

Has this short introduction to clicker training got you hooked? Do you think you could teach your hamster other behaviors with a clicker? Unfortunately, not a lot has been written about how to clicker-train small animals. There are a few web sites with useful information, but most books and web sites are geared to training dogs, birds, and cats. However, with a little ingenuity, you can adapt some of the techniques used in these guides and apply them to your hamster.

Chapter Fifteen
Leash Walking

Is leash walking possible?

A hamster on a leash? Is this even possible? Well, it isn't for dwarf hamsters. They're too small and squirmy to be harnessed up. But it's a different story for Syrian hamsters. Some Syrians take quite readily to leash walking . . . you can see videos on the Internet of Syrians that are enjoying a stroll. You can even find harnesses and leashes designed just for hamsters on the pet-store shelves and on Internet store or auction sites.

Why would you want to leash-walk a hamster? If you don't have time for hamster proofing or if you don't have a suitable room for hamster playtime, leash walking could be a good way for your pet to get some exercise.

Invest in a hamster harness

Before getting started, you'll have to find a hamster harness—a

Never try leash walking with dwarf hamsters, they're too tiny.

collar won't do. Your pet could slip out of it if it's too loose, or choke if it's too tight. And any harness you buy should be made specifically for hamsters. Ferret, guinea pig, or kitten harnesses are all too big. As for a leash, all hamster harnesses come with a matching leash.

Don't try to put a harness on your pet until he knows you well and is used to being handled. After all, being harnessed is a new experience for him. If you rush him into it, you could be bitten. (Tip: A treat will keep him busy while you're fastening the straps.) Fit the harness carefully: too loose and he'll escape; too tight and he'll be uncomfortable. You should just

be able to squeeze the tip of your baby finger under the strap. Be particularly careful when harnessing a Teddy Bear or Angora hamster. With these extra-furry hamsters, you need to fit the harness to the body and not to the fur. To make sure you've got the fit right, let your pet take his first tentative steps in an enclosed area (like the play place). Then, if he wriggles loose, he won't be able to escape.

Speaking of wriggling, if your hamster is very squirmy and makes it clear that he doesn't want to wear a harness, then take your cue from him and don't force the issue. It's better to have a happy hamster than a harnessed hamster.

Leash walking step-by-step

What spot in your house will make a good walking track? Think hall, mudroom, bathroom, or any uncarpeted room that can be closed off in case of escape.

Now for some leash-walking tips. Always walk your pet in the evening when he's more likely to cooperate. And let him walk where *he* wants to walk—he can't be trained to walk, sit, or heel like a dog. Guide him gently without yanking on the leash, or lifting him off the floor . . . you don't want to hurt him. And never leave a leashed hamster tied to a doorknob while you go and answer the phone.

Start with short walks. A few minutes at a time are enough until your hamster gets the hang of things. Gradually increase the time spent leash walking, until your pet is getting a good workout each day.

Never force your hamster either into a harness or into leash walking. Some hamsters want nothing to do with the whole idea. If your pet shows obvious signs of disliking leash walking, better forget the idea altogether and go to a playpen.

Is a hamster safe outdoors?

Although you'll see videos on the Internet of hamsters being walked outside, this is not a great idea.

Harnesses are not 100 percent escape-proof, and if your pet slips out of a harness, he will almost certainly find a way to slip out of your yard. Also, in most neighborhoods, there are roaming cats and predatory birds on the lookout for an easy meal. The bottom line is, if you walk your pet outside, you can't guarantee his safety.

Is there any way, then, that your hamster can get a breath of fresh air? Here's an idea. On a quiet, mild, still evening, how about taking your hamster's cage out to the deck, patio, or balcony? There, you and your pet can relax together—you in a lounge chair, and your hamster in his cage. DO NOT, under any circumstances, take him out of the cage . . . he could jump out of your hands and run off. DO NOT leave him alone without supervision . . . the weather could change, and he could get a chill or heatstroke. Your aim is not to give your pet unlimited outdoor time; it's just to let him enjoy a breath of fresh air.

Chapter Sixteen
The Traveling Hamster

Keep hamster travel to a minimum

Hamsters are creatures of habit—they're not usually too thrilled about traveling. In fact, the unfamiliar sights and sounds connected with travel can raise their stress levels. And remember, a stressed hamster can quickly become an ill hamster. It's better not to take your hamster traveling if you can avoid it. However, sometimes you won't have a choice. For example, you might have to take a sick hamster to the veterinarian. Or, you might be moving to a new home on the other side of the country and taking your hamster with you. For those times when a trip can't be avoided, here are some tips to make the journey as stress-free as possible.

Short car trips

A short car trip or taxi ride to the veterinarian is probably going to be the extent of most hamster travel. For short trips like this, what you'll need is a small-pet travel carrier or a small module or transport unit from your pet's cage setup.

Unfortunately, none of these units is designed for use with a seat belt, and this could be a safety issue. For example, if you make a sudden stop, or if you're involved in an accident, a handheld or an unsecured pet carrier could fly out of a passenger's hands or off the seat and be thrown around the inside of the car. This could cause injury to your pet or to the vehicle occupants. To transport your hamster safely, you should really put

Long car trips

Suppose you have to move across the country, and you're going by car. To get your hamster through the trip with minimal hassle, check out the following hamster-travel advice.

On a long trip, your pet needs some room to roam around. Forget the small module or carrier that you use for short trips; it will be too cramped. Instead, use a large modular-cage section or a good-sized, plastic storage box with ventilation holes drilled into the lid. Unfortunately, neither of these travel-cage options can be *safely* secured with a seat belt, so you'll have to put the travel cage into a dog or cat carrier that *can* be safely secured (see previous section). Just make sure that you can fit the storage box or module inside the carrier—you'll probably need to get a dog or cat carrier that comes in two sections so that you can lift off the top section to get the hamster travel cage inside.

Stock the travel cage with some of the comforts of home. For example, put in lots of soft bedding, some chew sticks, and a pile of fresh food in one corner. But don't put in a food bowl, a ceramic sleep house, or a potty; these could move around during the journey and injure your pet. And don't leave a water bottle in the cage, either. It could leak. Even worse, your hamster could break a tooth if she's sipping when the car hits a bump or pothole. The best way to take

the small-pet travel carrier into a dog or cat carrier that is specifically designed to be secured with a seat belt. To keep the small-pet carrier from bouncing around inside the larger carrier, pack towels into the space between the two carriers. And to prevent your hamster from munching on the towels, place sections of cardboard between the smaller carrier and the towels.

For a short trip, your pet won't need food or water. But why not put in a small piece of melon or cucumber so she'll have something juicy and thirst quenching to munch on? A hidden treat or gnaw stick will help keep her mind off the journey, too. And to help her feel safe, be sure to put plenty of cozy bedding in the carrier so that she can snuggle right in.

One last point . . . before putting your hamster into the car, check the weather. Is there a chill in the air? Then preheat the car. Is the weather really hot? Then cool the car down.

care of your pet's thirst when in the car is to put a piece of cucumber into the cage while you're traveling. Then, when you pull into a rest stop or service station, put your hamster's water bottle back into the cage while the car is parked.

The most important rule of the road is to never get a traveling hamster out of her carrier. Hamsters are known for quick getaways. And think of the chaos in the car if a hamster were on the loose! Avoid this potentially dangerous situation by confining your hamster to her carrier while the car is in motion.

Most people drive long distances in the daytime, just when hamsters need their rest. So be considerate: no loud music in the van and no bickering in the backseat. Your pet needs peace and quiet when she's snoozing.

If your travel plans involve overnight stays, your hamster needs to be in the motel with you, not out in the car by herself. It's best to call ahead to reserve a room in a pet-friendly motel. You probably won't have too much trouble finding places that will allow your hamster in the room with you. Hamsters don't bark, squawk, or meow, so they won't disturb other guests.

Remember, your hamster is lively and alert at night and in the early hours of the morning, just when you're trying to get some sleep, so put the hamster cage in the bathroom, and shut the door. This way you won't be disturbed by any overnight rustling or running.

Temperature warnings

Whether you're going on a short trip or a long trip with your hamster, always keep an eye on the weather. For example, heat can be life-threatening for a hamster. It doesn't take much time in an overheated environment for your pet to become a victim of heatstroke. Even on an overcast day, all that glass in a car can create a greenhouse effect, making the car an oven. Whenever the weather's hot outside, it's important to keep the car cool inside. Use that air-conditioning!

But what if your car or van doesn't have air-conditioning? If you're going on a short trip, you could call a taxi or a friend who has an air-conditioned car. On a longer trip, you could plan to travel in the mornings before it gets hot, or at night after the temperature has cooled down.

You should always keep the carrier out of the sun. Sunshades made for car windows are a big help here. They can be moved from window to window, depending on the direction of the sun's rays.

Another good solution is to create a microclimate around the carrier for your pet's comfort. Do this by taking some ice packs, wrapping them in towels, and stacking them around the travel carrier. Zip-lock freezer bags filled with ice cubes can be used, too, as can plastic water or soda bottles. Just fill them with water and freeze them.

Cold cars can cause problems for your pet as well. Your hamster is used to a comfortable house environment. If you stick her into an SUV that's been parked outside in freezing temperatures, she'll get chilled and could become sick. On cold winter days, warm up your vehicle before taking your pet for a ride in it. And always have something handy to throw over your hamster's carrier at either end of the journey—something warm, waterproof, or windproof, depending on the weather.

The stay-at-home hamster

When vacation time rolls around, most people like a change of scene. Hamsters, on the other hand, prefer their regular routine. For them, a trip away from home can be quite unnerving. This being the case, it's not a good idea to take your hamster along on your vacation travels—you should look into pet-sitting arrangements instead.

If you're just going away for a weekend, why not let your hamster look after herself? Stock her cage with plenty of nonperishable food, a few treats, and an extra sipper bottle (a single bottle could leak or get stopped up). Then leave her to pet-sit herself for a day or two. She'll be fine as long as she's in good health and living in an escape-proof cage. But just in case of an unexpected emergency, it's a good idea to leave a key with a neighbor. After all, if there's a power outage, your hamster could roast without air-conditioning, or freeze without heat.

Are you planning to be gone longer than a weekend? Then you could ask a friend, relative, or neighbor to look in on your hamster . . . preferably in the evening when she's up and about. The point is to keep your pet's daily routine as normal as possible. *You* don't disrupt your pet's sleep by changing her food, water, and bedding in the daytime— neither should your pet sitter.

If it's not convenient for an obliging friend or relative to visit your house on a daily basis, maybe he or she could take your hamster in as a guest. An away-from-home stay isn't the best pet-sitting solution for a hamster because hamsters don't like change, but you can ease your pet's apprehension by taking along her whole cage setup, or as much of it as your pet sitter has space for. Take along a supply of your pet's usual food, water, and bedding, as well as her favorite toys. And, give your pet sitter instructions on how and when to handle your hamster.

If you're new to a neighborhood, or if you don't want to impose on a friend or relative, a professional pet sitter could be the answer. You could ask your veterinarian for a recommendation, or you could check on the Internet to find professional pet sitters in your area. You could also look in your local newspaper or on the bulletin board at your neighborhood pet store. For your peace of mind, make sure that anyone you choose is licensed, bonded, and insured.

Whether your hamster is having a home-stay or an away-stay, give the sitter a detailed list of care instructions. Include food require-

ments, your veterinarian's phone number, the after-hours emergency clinic's phone number, and your cell phone number. Tell your sitter what steps to take if your hamster has a medical emergency. Spell out exactly how much you can afford for emergency veterinary care. If the estimated costs are going to be higher, ask the sitter to call you for instructions.

It's not usually a good idea to take a hamster to a pet-boarding facility such as a kennel, a pet store, or a veterinary clinic. Barking, screeching, yowling, clanging doors, ringing phones, overly bright lights, and unfamiliar smells can stress out a hamster. Don't even consider any facility that can't guarantee that your pet will be kept by herself in a quiet location. And if you do find one that guarantees a quiet setting for your hamster, go check it out for yourself. Don't take someone else's word for it.

Chapter Seventeen
Handy Hints

Hamsters and other pets

You already know that Syrian hamsters are loners and should never share a cage with another hamster. And although some dwarf species can have a companion or two, sometimes that doesn't even work out. What about keeping other small rodents such as rats or gerbils with a hamster? Forget it. Keeping different species together in the same cage just doesn't work. One of the animals is likely to get hurt or killed.

What about letting your hamster(s) interact with larger household pets, like cats or dogs? Don't do it! Outside the cage, a hamster could be injured or killed by a larger pet. But even inside the cage, a hamster could be traumatized by the presence of a barking dog or a prowling cat. Keep your hamster and his cage in a separate room where he won't be frightened and stressed by other, larger pets.

Don't let other pets near your hamster's cage. It's too stressful for the hamster.

Grooming

The good news about grooming is that hamsters take care of this chore themselves. In fact, grooming is a big part of a happy and contented hamster's daily routine. He'll lick his paws, comb through his fur, and wash his face—over and over again. You might need to give a hand to a long-haired or angora hamster if bedding gets stuck in his fur. But even then, it's just a matter of a quick brush with a soft-bristled toothbrush or pet brush. As for baths, hamsters don't need them. In fact, baths are not good for hamsters; their furry little bodies take a long time to dry, and bathing puts them at risk of catching a cold. However, many hamsters do enjoy a sand bath in chinchilla sand (see Chapter 11).

There's no need to clean a hamster's ears, brush his teeth, or clip his claws. He looks after his ears himself during his grooming routine. You help him to keep his teeth clean and trimmed to the right length by supplying him with chew toys (gnawing is nature's answer to dental care). You can also help him keep his nails short by placing a plain old brick or flat stone in the cage under the food dish. This way, your hamster has to climb onto the brick or stone every time he wants a mouthful of food, and the rough surface helps to keep his nails trimmed.

If, however, your pet's nails do get too long, please take him to the veterinarian to have them clipped. And if his incisors grow too long or become misshapen, again, take your pet to a veterinarian. Tooth trimming and nail clipping are not jobs for an owner to tackle.

Catching an escaped hamster

It's a well-known fact that hamsters are escape artists. Many of them manage to get out of their cages by slithering through the bars or gnawing a hole in the plastic. Don't be fooled by your hamster's chunky-looking body. He can get through a very small space, and once on the loose, he can move fast and evade cap-

ture. If this happens, how are you going to track him down and get him back?

First, narrow the search by figuring out which room he's in. How? Get out some sunflower seeds and lay out a little pile of 10 seeds on the floor of each room in your house or apartment. Close the doors to every room, and stuff any gap between door and floor with rolled-up towels. Then every few hours, do the rounds and check for missing seeds—an escaped hamster is bound to get hungry sooner or later. The room with the missing seeds is the room with the missing hamster.

Now that you know where your hamster is, how do you capture him? In fact, how do you even find him? He could be holed up anywhere: under the furniture, in the plants, in the bookcase, inside the sofa bed, or under a pillow. Check the obvious hidey-holes first. No luck? Try putting a travel cage or a plastic module from his cage system into the room at floor level. The scent of his home might be enough to lure him in. Chances are, it won't be long before you find him snoozing soundly in his sleep house. If you don't, it's time to set a trap.

Many books and Internet sites recommend putting a ramp up to a bucket, and baiting both with sunflower seeds or a favorite treat. The idea is for the hamster to follow the treats up the ramp and then jump into the bucket to get some more seeds. This seems like a good idea because a hungry hamster is liable

to follow a food trail, and once inside the bucket he won't be able get out again. But there's a problem with this strategy: a hamster could get injured falling into the bucket. So, cover the bottom of the bucket with a thick layer of cushy nesting material for a soft landing. P.S. The seed bait needs to go on top of the bedding, not underneath the bedding on the bottom of the bucket.

Are there any other ways to recapture a truant hamster? You could buy or rent a live small-animal trap. Don't be put off by the word *trap*. These devices don't hurt or maim pets. They're designed to catch an animal alive and keep it alive until you release it. How do they work? You place food, water, and bedding inside the trap. Sooner or later, the hungry and thirsty runaway smells the bait and heads in to investigate, and the door shuts behind it.

Of course, preventing an escape is better than dealing with one. So, check your hamster's cage weekly for signs of wear and tear. Lock down or tape down the lids of all cage add-ons. And always close the cage doors tightly. Also, keep the door to the hamster's room closed. This way, if he does escape, he'll be confined to one room.

Chapter Eighteen
Making the Grade

"A" for effort

Well done! You've worked hard at training, and now you and your hamster have made the grade. Thanks to your patience and perseverance, your pet has learned to come when you knock or whistle, she's learned to use a potty, and she's learned to run an obstacle course. With your help, your hamster's brain is being challenged by a variety of entertaining toys, and she's being stimulated by regular out-of-the-cage playtime. She's getting down to daily fitness training, too, because you've turned her cage into an exercise center with running wheel, ramps, seesaws, and tunnels.

You hamster has also learned the social skills she needs to be a great family pet. Most important, she has learned to take a relaxed approach to life with humans . . . she is HAPPY.

Learning is for life

Now that you've taken all the time and effort to train your hamster, don't slack off. You need to keep up the good work if your pet is to keep on her toes. Too many hamster owners neglect their pets after the initial novelty has worn off. Don't let this happen in your house. For your pet to stay happy and healthy, she needs your wholehearted commitment, day after day after day.

Useful Information

Hamsters (Animal Planet Pet Care Library)
Author: Sue Fox
Publisher: TFH Publications Inc. (September 2006)

Hamsters for Dummies
Author: Sarah Montague
Publisher: For Dummies; 1st edition (April 30, 2007)

Dwarf Hamsters (Complete Pet Owner's Manual)
Author: Sharon Vanderlip
Publisher: Barron's Educational Series; 1st edition (March 2009)

Hamsterlopaedia: A Complete Guide to Hamster Care
Authors: Chris Logsdail, Peter Logsdail, and Kate Hovers
Publisher: Interpet Publishing (February 2004)

Hamsters (A Complete Pet Owner's Manual)
Author: Peter Fritzsche
Publisher: Barron's Educational Series, Inc.; 2nd edition (May 1, 2008)

There are many reputable web sites on the Internet that contain very useful information about Syrian and dwarf hamsters. However, it's not practical to list them here because web sites come and go, or sometimes change their web site addresses.

Try typing the following key words into a few search engines:
- Syrian hamsters
- Dwarf hamsters
- Djungarian hamsters
- Campbell's dwarf hamsters
- Siberian dwarf hamsters
- Roborovski dwarf hamsters
- Chinese dwarf hamsters
- Chinese hamsters
- Clicker training
- Clicker training small pets
- Lure-reward training

Index